PRAISE FOR *BE DATA*

'Data literacy is one of the world's top job skills today and in the future, and Jordan Morrow knows everything there is to know about the topic. If you want to boost the data literacy of yourself or your team, then start with this book!'
Bernard Marr, world-renowned futurist, influencer and thought leader in business and technology

'Jordan Morrow is *the* face of data literacy. In this debut book, his passion for the subject shines through, conveying clear messages on improved data literacy, data-driven strategies and better decision-making. A must-read for data specialists, business executives and more!
Christina Stathopoulos, Data Specialist, Google and Adjunct Professor, IE Business School

'Get ready for a guided tour on data literacy. Jordan Morrow has put together a must-have book on what it means to be data literate, and provides clear steps to take you on your very own data literacy journey.'
Kate Strachnyi, Founder, Story by Data, DATAcated Academy and DATAcated Conference

'Data literacy is a popular term in the business world these days, but both the concept and its value are often vaguely articulated. In this engaging and effective book, Jordan Morrow is clear about what the individual needs to know, but he also draws on broad industry experience to map out a strategic path for organizations and teams. Whether you're an executive wishing your business was better informed, or an individual analyst trying to better explain and persuade with data, you'll find valuable examples and tactical models here.'
Donald Farmer, Principal, Treehive Strategy

'Jordan Morrow has created an instant classic. This book highlights why he is called "The Godfather of Data Literacy". He effectively translates his vast experience and expertise into a playbook that people can use to develop their data literacy skills in a logical and pragmatic manner. From clarity around the steps of the data literacy process to how we can make better, more informed decisions using the power of data, he serves as your guide on the path towards data literacy. Read this book and develop your data superpowers.'
Jason Krantz, Founder and CEO, Strategy Titan

'Data literacy is not a science or a math skill. It is a life skill, achievable by everyone. This excellent book covers every dimension of data literacy, from being to doing, starting with the most basic human aptitude: being curious! This book will build from there, to data fluency and data brilliance. Everyone can navigate that journey with this remarkably rewarding book.'
Kirk Borne, PhD, Principal Data Scientist, Data Science Fellow, and Executive Advisor, Booz Allen Hamilton

'Data literacy is an absolutely critical skill for today's workforce. Not just to meet the current needs, but also to set individuals and organizations up for the future of work. This book gives a thorough understanding of what data literacy is, why it is important today, and how to learn to become more data literate. It is full of very useful and practical tips and strategies that can be applied across both your work and personal life as you interact more with data. I highly recommend this book to anyone looking to learn more about what data literacy is and trying to increase their overall data literacy.'
Kevin Hanegan, Chief Learning Officer, Qlik

Be Data Literate

*The Data Literacy Skills Everyone Needs
To Succeed*

Jordan Morrow

KoganPage

Publisher's note

Every possible effort has been made to ensure that the information contained in this book is accurate at the time of going to press, and the publishers and author cannot accept responsibility for any errors or omissions, however caused. No responsibility for loss or damage occasioned to any person acting, or refraining from action, as a result of the material in this publication can be accepted by the editor, the publisher or the author.

First published in Great Britain and the United States in 2021 by Kogan Page Limited

2nd Floor, 45 Gee Street	122 W 27th St, 10th Floor	4737/23 Ansari Road
London	New York, NY 10001	Daryaganj
EC1V 3RS	USA	New Delhi 110002
United Kingdom		India

www.koganpage.com

Kogan Page books are printed on paper from sustainable forests.

ISBNs

Hardback   978 1 78966 803 2
Paperback   978 1 78966 801 8
Ebook   978 1 78966 802 5

British Library Cataloguing-in-Publication Data

A CIP record for this book is available from the British Library.

Library of Congress Cataloging-in-Publication Data

Names: Morrow, Jordan, author.
Title: Be data literate : the data literacy skills everyone needs to succeed / Jordan Morrow.
Description: London ; New York, NY : KoganPage, 2021. | Includes
   bibliographical references and index.
Identifiers: LCCN 2020050697 (print) | LCCN 2020050698 (ebook) | ISBN
   9781789668032 (hardback) | ISBN 9781789668018 (paperback) | ISBN
   9781789668025 (ebook)
Subjects: LCSH: Data mining. | Research–Data processing. | Quantitative
   research. | Information literacy.
Classification: LCC QA76.9.D343 M68 2021 (print) | LCC QA76.9.D343
   (ebook) | DDC 006.3/12–dc23
LC record available at https://lccn.loc.gov/2020050697
LC ebook record available at https://lccn.loc.gov/2020050698

Typeset by Integra Software Services, Pondicherry
Print production managed by Jellyfish
Printed and bound by CPI Group (UK) Ltd, Croydon CR0 4YY

To my beautiful wife and five wonderful children. Thank you for your support in my journey with data literacy.

CONTENTS

LIST OF FIGURES

ABOUT THE AUTHOR

Jordan Morrow is known as the 'Godfather of Data Literacy'. Seen as one of the founders and pioneers of the data literacy movement, Jordan Morrow has a passion to help organizations achieve their data and analytical potential. When not found in the world of data literacy, Jordan Morrow is a family man, happily married with five children. Jordan is also an avid trail and ultra-marathon runner. He can often be found in the mountains near his home.

PREFACE

There are three types of lies – lies, damn lies, and statistics.[1]

This quote, unfortunately misattributed to multiple people, such as Mark Twain, tells the story of our lives right now. We live in a world where statistics, data, information, numbers, words, and so many other things (including pictures at times) are shared to tell us stories and convey information. Is it easy for us to understand all the data and information presented to us on a regular basis? Unfortunately, they are often misused and misrepresented with efficacy. Is there something we can do about this?

I started my journey into the world of data literacy officially in June of 2016, but my first ideas were rolling before then. I have been given the nicknames of the Godfather of Data Literacy and Chief Nerd Officer (I really like the second nickname). Over time, I have developed, improved, and evolved my thinking and thought process around data literacy. This book is here to convey my thoughts and help you on your data literacy, data, and analytics journey.

This book will take a different approach than what you may expect from a book that deals with such topics of data and analytics. For most of us, these topics are not at the top of our list of exciting or thrilling subjects, but to me they are fascinating. I hope to convey to you a strong understanding of the world of data literacy and what you can do to take part in this exciting time where the world is truly data driven. Thank you for taking the time to sit down with me. I hope to spark in you a curiosity and love of data literacy in the hope it will truly impact your life for the better, as it has for me.

Note

1 Anon. (2012) Lies, damned lies and statistics, University of York. Available at: www.york.ac.uk/depts/maths/histstat/lies.htm (archived at perma.cc/4RY4-THZX)

01

The world of data

Have you ever wondered to yourself: what does the future look like? What will the job market be like, and are robots and technology truly going to monopolize and take my job away? What inventions await us, and, maybe most importantly, when will my flying car arrive? The future will always be uncertain, and inventions that shape the future will certainly be things we haven't even thought of or created yet. It is an undeniable fact that there will be jobs in the future that we can't begin to imagine. Even though we have all these different uncertainties, there is one thing that we know will be part of the future and is already here: data. The future promises to bring about many waves of inventions and exciting new jobs, but while we wait on those things, we do know that the power of data is here. The fact is, data is here to stay.

The world of data is amazing, vast, and provides countless growth opportunities for individuals. For far too long, individuals and organizations have been halted in their attempts to drive success with data. That should no longer be the case and we must help everyone to capitalize on this vast asset.

Data has been called the 'new oil', as lifesaving as water, and many other clichéd and over-hyped terms. The reality is, data is truly an asset and when used properly it can help everyone move forward and succeed. It can help us to develop stronger understanding and knowledge, prepare our résumés to handle the future, and build within everyone a strong and versatile foundation for the future. This foundational understanding of the world of data is essential.

Data: The world we live in

It is no secret – we are living in a world consumed by technology and data. One can hardly walk down the streets of big cities like London or New York and find people who are not looking down at their phones versus up at the amazing sites and people around them. Take a personal test: next time you are walking in a big city, count how many people are looking down at their phone versus looking up. You can even add up those talking or waving hello. Also, don't forget to look up yourself, saving yourself from a potentially bad trip over a curb or, worse yet, having a nasty run-in with a local vehicle.

Over the last 50 years, and particularly the last 30 years with the advent of the internet, personal computers, smart phones, and so forth, the world has seen amazing advancements in the growth of technology and data. Ponder on those advancements for just a moment. When one looks at the expanse of time, with the universe being around 13.8 billion years old,[1] and the Earth itself around 4.5 billion years old,[2] we are talking just about 30–50 years. In these 30–50 years, we have seen where personal computers and cell phones have become mainstream. This time period is not even a sliver on the scale that is time. Now, for us in our day and age, it is hard to imagine these items not being a part of life. Each one of these items is data producing. What about the internet? The internet is even younger, gaining mainstream life in the early 1990s,[3] and really taking off in the late 1990s. Now the internet is ubiquitous to jobs and life itself. With all this growth in personal computing, technology has sped up in its development and not slowed down. We continually see innovation, advancement, and different aspects of the digital world evolve and expand. All of this has a direct impact on our lives, the way we live, and so forth. Above all, with respect to the topic at hand, all this has an effect on the life and power of data.

Take the more impassioned use of the internet when it went mainstream. The internet changed the way organizations, schools, and our lives operated. Our way of life not only changed, but vastly improved; the internet allowed us to improve, learn, and develop at unprecedented rates. When one combined the internet with the personal computer, and now the even more powerful personal computer we call smart phones, individuals and families could bring the power of computers into a home. People could bring more than the entirety of the Encyclopedia Britannica, minus the door-to-door salesperson, into their lives. Not only bring it into their lives, they could get answers to their questions much faster. This has evolved in what we know today as Google, with 'google' becoming a verb in the Merriam-Webster dictionary![4]

As this digital advancement continued, we saw the growth in e-commerce and the birth of companies like Amazon changing consumer habits and monopolizing the market. We saw the rise and fall of the internet bubble, where companies that had no business being valued highly, were valued at enormous sums. One prime example of this was Pets.com. Pets.com was started in 1998 and shuttered its doors in 2000.[5] With the fall of the internet bubble, different kinds of internet sites came into existence, and the world was introduced to the world of social media. Social media has opened the gates on consumer profiles, making their digital and data worlds public for everyone to see, from selfies and pictures of our food, to what products we are enjoying. All of this is consumable data available to both individuals and enterprises. Because we all want the targeted advertisement making the decision for what we want for dinner this evening!

Along with the advent of social media, and all the fun data it is producing for us, the 2000s saw a new type of technology come to the forefront of connectivity and data collection: the Internet of Things, or IoT. A definition of the IoT is easy: a connectedness of everything. Think of sensors on a car or plane collecting information and data on what is going on with the engine or other parts. A quick question, though: Did the IoT really start in the 2000s? The answer is no, and many will not know this. The term gained its official name in 1999, but one of the first examples of the IoT was found in a simple item that most of us cross or have crossed regularly for years: a Coca-Cola vending machine. The particular vending machine we are talking about was found at Carnegie Melon University. At this vending machine, individuals would connect to the refrigerated appliance by the internet and discover if a drink was cold before going to the machine and purchasing said drink.[6] This use of data to make a smarter decision, through connectedness, ie the IoT, has been on the minds of people for years: how do we use the information and data we are collecting to improve decision-making in our lives and careers? Think of enterprises like Amazon or Netflix: how often are they collecting our data to 'make recommendations' on what we want? Often... and guess what? They are right with these recommendations a lot of the time.

Although the IoT starting to form back in the 1980s, it wasn't until recent years when the world of the IoT gained the steam and momentum we have come to know it by. For example, picture a trail runner who loves running ultra-marathons. When the runner is on the trail or road running, a few years ago there wasn't that much technology around to collect data and information to help the runner grow... and we can say help a runner 'grow' lightly. Do we really need a watch that shows you every single possible aspect of a run: from elevation, to pace, to feet ascended and descended? The data in front of runners today captures more information than they probably need, providing pages and pages to swipe through! The watch data is such a fun example of items we can read through and discuss, but there is one key element to all of this that is occurring in our world today: the connectivity around us and the advancement of technology are producing more and more data in our lives. What are some other real-world examples of the IoT? What are examples where we are seeing advancements or things evolving in ways that help, shape, and decide our lives?

One example of a company harnessing the connectivity, digitization, and production of data is the great company Rolls-Royce. Rolls-Royce is no longer just a great engineering company, producing amazing engines. Now, Rolls-Royce is a powerful, data-driven organization that utilizes the IoT and connectivity to deliver and produce data that is an essential asset to its company.[7] An example of Rolls-Royce utilizing the power of data is their predictive forecasting method to monitoring engine maintenance.[8] By using sensors and the information they produce, Rolls-Royce is mastering how to predict and anticipate any issues that may arise with their aircraft engines, and ensure they keep planes in the air. Another prime example of the connectivity of things empowering our lives can be found within healthcare. Utilizing data and information produced through physical therapy appointments provides better physical therapy programs that can be designed for those in need.[9] With the rising cost of healthcare, more direct and prescriptive services can help individuals feel better and stay out of the hospital.

The world of sports is another area that has developed and grown massively through the world of data and analytics. How many of us have heard of or seen the movie *Moneyball* starring the ever-amazing Brad Pitt? That movie showed us that data and analytics can greatly influence a sports team, helping drive wins for a smaller baseball market. One great example of this can be found in the international sport of basketball, particularly the National Basketball Association (NBA). Most, if not all, NBA teams have hired data analysts and experts. These experts are tasked with finding trends and patterns in the information they are collecting, such as finding undervalued players and creating value for trades and other options. Another way NBA teams are utilizing data and technology is to monitor fatigue and sleep levels, allowing them to understand how to address training, prevent injuries, etc. One of the fun ways that the NBA is utilizing data and analytics is by hosting an annual hackathon, helping the NBA to find talented new analysts. Did you know that data analysis is largely credited with the increase in 3-point shooting in the league?[10]

It's not just the NBA that gets to have all the fun. Everyday objects are now capable of harnessing the power of data, such as smart watches, smart phones, dishwashers, refrigerators, heating and air conditioning systems, cars and vehicles, and more. Along with all these products and tools, many other areas are producing data at unbelievable rates. Think of all the information being produced through social media sites, visits to e-commerce sites like Amazon or Ebay, swipes of credit cards, and more. Overall, we are seeing some amazing numbers with data production each day. The World Economic Forum stated in 2019:[11]

- 500 million daily tweets are sent;
- 294 billion emails are sent;
- 4 terabytes of data are created from each connected car;
- by 2025, it's estimated that 463 exabytes of data will be created each day globally.

If we were all still watching DVDs regularly and not Netflix, that would be the equivalent of 212,765,957 DVDs. Wow, that is an unbelievable amount of data! What does that mean for us? It means we cannot watch all the DVDs our data producing is creating. What can we do with all that information?

Surely organizations and individuals are capitalizing on this amazing asset of data, right? Obviously, organizations are not falling short and are able to find insight to make smart, data informed decisions, aren't they? The reality says quite differently, and studies and data show us the truth: there is a large skills gap in the world of data that is hurting organizations' ability to succeed with their own valuable assets of data and analytical investments.

Data: The skills gap

To understand this large skills gap, one needs to understand the overall data skills landscape. The data and analytics firm Qlik helped all of us to understand the world's current data skills landscape and where there may be gaps in those skills. One research study, conducted from August 2017 through February 2018 showed the overall data literacy and data skills landscape, providing valuable insight into people and their skill level and comfort in using data.[12] The results were staggering. In the study, it was found that just 24 per cent of decision-makers felt confident in their data literacy, or data skills. Just 24 per cent! That is a staggeringly low number for those tasked with leading decisions in organizations. In some cases, these same decision-makers are tasked with or making data-driven decisions. With that large a gap, should we trust those decisions?

When organizations are setting their data and analytical strategy (which hopefully they have, but trends say otherwise) they look to the executive team to formulate, empower, and give direction so they can strategize and plan to utilize data to make their business better. Well, through the same research and study, guess what proportion of the executive team was confident in their skills to use data? Thirty-two per cent! That is just about 1 out of 3 in the executive level, and if we really had to assess this, that level would be a bit too high; I would venture that the executive level is below 32 per cent in their true ability to utilize data and in their data literacy level. If the c-suite are determining the data vision and strategy of an organization, it is up to that 24 per cent of decision-makers to implement said strategy and vision. How can a decision-maker with low confidence in their data skills be tasked with actually implementing this effectively? One can start to see the issues with the skills gap.

What about those entering the workforce right now, the younger age group? The same Qlik study and research found that with the lower age group, the group aged 16 to 24, only 21 per cent were confident in their data and data literacy abilities. This low number for the younger age group can lead one to ask: how is this age group not confident in their data literacy skills? Aren't they naturally or already confident with data? This is a very interesting question that requires a deeper look at that age demographic. Those in the age demographic of 18 to 24 as of 2017 (when the study was carried out) were born in the digital world, when the internet and personal computers were a ubiquitous part of life. This group has been raised by technology, social media, and the internet... but that does not mean they have been raised to utilize the world of data and analytics. This group is very digitally literate, not data literate.

Overall, about 1 out of 5 participants in the study was confident in their data literacy skills, leaving a massive gap for organizations to fill. This is where the problem sits: if organizations are looking to capitalize on data and analytics, but there is a massive skills gap, how can they capitalize? Also, what sort of impact is this lack of data literacy and confidence with data having on organizations? Is it potentially hitting the bottom line?

The human impact of data literacy and the skills gap cannot be overstated. In a study conducted in 2019, it was found that only 32 per cent of 'business executives surveyed said that they're able to create measurable value from data, while just 27 per cent said their data and analytics projects produce actionable insights'.[13] Again, this is a direct tie and flow to the lack of data literacy skills in the world. When one thinks of the millions and millions, even billions, of dollars that are invested in data and analytical projects, software and technology, one must begin to wonder how much is being lost. When the overall population sits at 1 out of 5 having confidence in their data skills, and business executives are not realizing value, the loss is potentially massive.

OK, so what kind of impact does lack of data literacy have on us, the individuals? The study showed us just how quantifiable this lack of data and analytical success is. When we dig into the study, we find individuals, because of this large skills gap, are becoming supremely overwhelmed by the amount of data and technology being presented to them. Over a third of the study's participants said they would find alternative methods to completing a task instead of using data, and 14 per cent said they would avoid it altogether. The more staggering outlook for being sick of and overwhelmed by data came in the form of hours of work lost per employee: five working days, or slightly more, at 43 hours lost per employee per year, because of being overwhelmed by and sick of data technology. How much does that cost in actual dollar amounts? Well, the number is not small. The study showed the cost to the U.S. economy accounted for US$100 billion. Do these numbers shock you? The question we need to ask ourselves now, is why are people so overwhelmed and why do we have this large skills gap?

Data: Why is there a skills gap?

With a large skills gap like this, there must be causes, right? There must be drivers causing this skills gap, but what are they? In the case of a large data skills gap, there are many options. These causes, drivers, or expanders of a skills gap take many forms, from education and schooling to technology and software issues, to the data production itself. As we unwrap these causes, think of how these have impacted your career and ability to utilize data and analytics for success, whether from a personal level or those people you have worked with.

Software and technology

One may ask: how can software and technology be a cause or driver of a data skills gap? Aren't software and technology here to help us? Aren't the advancements and improvements in software and technology decreasing the skills gap? Well, the answer to the last two questions is Yes! Software and technology are here to help us drive solutions and answers to data and analytics problems, generating business outcomes. In reality, software and technology are here to help augment humans, if we are trained and educated enough to let it happen.

The problem lies in the way the different investments in technology and software have been deployed by both individuals and enterprises. Imagine you are a company building a data and analytical strategy, designed to help you succeed with data in the digital and data revolution, and a great sales person comes by your office and says: 'Our new software is designed to assist and empower you to truly succeed with your data and analytical needs.' What if they say: 'Our software will solve all your data and analytical needs.' They can throw any number of awesome phrases at you to buy their software. You get to see the perfect examples and case studies broadcast across their laptops or screens. With those perfect examples, you decide and invest in this software and look to roll it out to the masses. When organizations roll out data and analytical software to the masses, this is called the 'democratization of data', and, a little secret, the democratization of data is what companies should be doing but is also a problem. Let's examine this more.

Historically, data would reside in the information and technology world or another part of the business, with a few people using the data or producing the reports and analyses; the organization was reliant on that team to produce strong, applicable results. As business intelligence tools, like Qlik or Tableau, advanced and grew into powerhouse software companies, organizations looked to spread the data to the masses, thereby democratizing the data and information. When an organization democratizes data to the masses, the organization is hoping to drive strong insights and results. There is one large problem with this: how many of us go to school and university to develop skills in data, analytics, mathematics, statistics, and so forth? This number has risen in recent years with the rise in emphasis on STEM (science, technology, engineering, and math) education, but what about all those who did not go to school for this type of education?

It may seem like we are saying democratizing data is not the answer… wrong! Democratizing data to the masses is the answer – it is how organizations can realize more potential through data and analytical investment. Democratizing data allows the unique talents and abilities of an enterprise's workforce to capitalize on the investments the organization has made in software, data, and technology. The reason democratizing data has expanded the skills gap lies in the educational foundations of an enterprise's workforce. When individuals without backgrounds in data and technology are asked to take on new software and technology and to capitalize on data and information, those people are not effectively prepared to utilize the data in front of them. How many of us do you think are eager and happy to jump in to use these new investments? How often are you excited to jump in and learn something thrust upon you and your job?

The same study from 2019 on the human impact of data literacy stated that 36 per cent of study participants 'would find an alternative method to complete the task without using data', and 14 per cent of study participants 'would avoid the task entirely' rather than use data. This is indicative of a lack of data skills; those who are comfortable with and confident in using data are more comfortable with the investments made. In the same study, it was found that nearly three-quarters, or 74 per cent, of study participants felt overwhelmed by or unhappy working with data. This last metric shows the fatigue wearing on individuals when it comes to the investments and democratization of data. This overall fatigue and lack of skills to utilize data has truly expanded the data skills gap.

Data production

What would data production have to do with lack of data skills? Data production, as it pertains to what has been discussed, is not new but was covered earlier in the chapter. With the advent of technology and pace with which it grew, and the pace of data production accelerating, organizations and their workforces were not equipped to handle how quickly they were producing data. Those organizations that were born and bred during the digital era were more equipped to succeed with the onslaught of data, as it was a part of who they were. Those enterprises that were not started and built during the digital era? They are trying to build capabilities to use data effectively and are finding it more complicated. You mean I can't just start sourcing and using data? No! These enterprises are learning you can't just invest in software and technology, sourcing data, and poof, the entire enterprise is walking on top of the data and analytical mountain. What was found, on the other hand, were workforces unable to keep up with the rapidly changing environment. The quick onslaught of producing and sourcing data is a cause of the data skills gap.

Lack of data and analytical strategy

Another driver and cause of the data skills gap is the lack of data and analytical strategy within organizations. How can a lack of a strategy drive or expand a skills gap? To start, sit back and think to yourself: does my enterprise have a clear and concise data and analytical strategy? For a lot of enterprises, the unfortunate answer is 'No'. This lack of strategy can put undue burdens on the workforce, who are just trying to figure out how to utilize and adopt the software and technology invested in (remember our study from 2019? That overwhelming feeling is real!).

What does it mean for an enterprise to have a clear and concise data and analytical strategy? Let's take this to a personal example of needing a strategy by jumping back to running a half-marathon, marathon, or ultra-marathon. To help, let's emphasize this is a beginner or intermediate level runner running the race.

First, imagine you are this runner. You haven't run for a very long time and you see some of your friends, family, or coworkers taking on this task of running a race. You see them get super excited about it, and, let's face it, sometimes they don't stop talking about it (as a runner myself, I know I talk about it way too much). You decide then and there you are going to sign up for a race and toe the starting line. You then sign up for your first race, and it officially starts in a few months. You signed up for this race without a training strategy, not studying the racecourse, getting to know your nutrition or hydration needs, but you train and eat knowing you need to. Without the strategy, you also don't know if that investment is giving you the return you desire.

It's then time for the race. You toe the starting line with some training under your belt. Maybe you have some hydration or nutrition, just hopeful the training you have completed will get you through. The starting timer goes off and the race turns out to be a disaster. You weren't properly prepared, even though you did some training and bought some equipment. In the case of a half-marathon, you get to the finish but really struggle through. For both the full and ultra-marathons, you fall short and do not finish.

Now, contrast this with another race. You sign up, after building a strategy for the event. You know the equipment you need, the hydration and nutrition your body needs, and you hire the right coach to help guide you through the strategy. In fact, this coach helped you build the strategy. There are some bumps and hiccups along the way. In the end, you make it through challenging training and you are set for the race. When that day comes, you are able to get through the finish, even with some pain and frustration. At the end, you knew how to deal with it and succeed because of the strategy and preparation.

Overall, these examples spell out exactly what organizations need to do with data and analytical strategy. For far too long, some companies have gone the more haphazard route. They have known they need to invest in data and analytics, but only going partly in, not knowing what equipment and why they are buying it or knowing if it fits the needs. They aren't using the 'coaches' they should to build the strategy and then implement said strategy. Then they find their investments they have made, in some cases millions of dollars, are falling flat and not giving a good return. Unfortunately, this is the issue many companies are facing.

A strong data and analytical strategy means the enterprise has built a strategy for sourcing and utilizing data and analytics to further the enterprise's goals, vision, and objectives. Trends from around the world are illuminating that most enterprises have not fully vetted strong data and analytical strategy.

When organizations around the world are not prepared with strong data and analytical strategies, this expands the data skills gap. Instead of having a clear strategy that dictates and allows the flow of software, technology, and learning investment, companies have purchased the data and analytical software and technology to do it all for them. In doing so, they are using the technology as the strategy itself, forcing it upon people. This does not allow the strategy to dictate what technology to use. This type of 'strategy' can result in weak adoption by the workforce; the workforce can then go back to the old way of doing things. When they go back to the old way of doing things, the new technology is like the toy placed on a shelf, collecting dust.

As such, organizations were hit with a double whammy: first, the software they have invested in is not being used and adopted effectively, and second, instead of the workforce growing in data skills, they are falling further behind as they push away from the investments and technology that was purchased for their benefit.

Data: What's next?

With a large skills gap, we can ask ourselves: ok, data isn't being used effectively, so what's the point? What's next? Do we really need to close this skills gap, or can we just keep marching along? To be blunt: we must close this skills gap!

As was stated earlier, we are looking at an estimated 463 exabytes of data by the year 2025. To give you an idea, besides DVDs, on just how much data that is: one exabyte of data is a 1 with 18 zeros behind it… that's 18 zeros. So imagine to yourself the number 463, then put 18 zeros behind it. A different prediction states there will be 175 zettabytes by 2025, which is 1 followed by 21 zeros; 1 zettabyte equates to a trillion gigabytes.[14] Now, which of these is right? Or is the better question: does it matter? This is a lot of data and it cannot be questioned that there is a lot of value and insight within these massive amounts of data. The problem again: if we have a large data skills gap, will individuals and enterprises be able to capitalize on this vast amount of data and information, or will we continue to see those organizations who can utilize data effectively surpass those organizations who cannot?

Chapter summary

Overall, the world of data we live in is exciting, scary, and unknown. The future holds many different jobs, opportunities, and inventions, and we cannot know what they entail. There will be needs for new skills, but we don't even know what they are. One thing is certain: data is here to stay! We have seen there are great trends of data growing, expanding, and needing to be utilized. We have also seen there is a large skills gap in the workforce of enterprises, also expanding and growing. This gap blocks the success of enterprise's data and analytical investment. What can be done, and are there answers to this? The answer is a resounding Yes! Many opportunities await those individuals and organizations who embrace the world of data literacy.

Notes

1 Redd, N (2017) How Old is the Universe, Space.com, 8 June. Available from: https://www.space.com/24054-how-old-is-the-universe.html (archived at perma.cc/K6LF-UCAL)

2 Redd, N (2017) How Old is the Universe, Space.com, 08 June. Available from: https://www.space.com/24054-how-old-is-the-universe.html (archived at perma.cc/94R7-GBJK)

3 Zimmerman, K & Emspak, J (2017) Internet History Timeline: ARPANET to the World Wide Web, Live Science, 27 June. Available from: https://www.livescience.com/20727-internet-history.html (archived at perma.cc/YLA9-RJNV)

4 Merriam-Webster Dictionary. Available from: https://www.merriam-webster.com/dictionary/google (archived at perma.cc/QSU7-3XNZ)

5 Aune, S (2010) Five Dot-Coms That Didn't Survive the Bubble, technoBuffalo, 25 January. Available from: https://www.technobuffalo.com/five-dot-coms-that-didnt-survive-the-bubble (archived at perma.cc/FUG6-LUCL)

6 Foote, K (2016) A Brief History of the Internet of Things, Dataversity.net, 16 August. Available from: https://www.dataversity.net/brief-history-internet-things/# (archived at perma.cc/TAQ2-3N2U)

7 Choudhury, A R and Mortleman, J (2018) How IoT is Turning Rolls-Royce into a Data Fuelled Business, CIO, January. Available from: https://www.i-cio.com/innovation/internet-of-things/item/how-iot-is-turning-rolls-royce-into-a-data-fuelled-business (archived at perma.cc/XYD3-ULN5)

8 RTInsights Team (2016) How Rolls-Royce Maintains Jet Engines With the IoT, RT insights.com, 11 October Available from: https://www.rtinsights.com/rolls-royce-jet-engine-maintenance-iot/ (archived at perma.cc/EGT6-L52R)

9 Medical Device Network (2018) Bringing the Internet of Things to Healthcare, MedicalDevice-Network.com, 3 September. Available from: https://www.medicaldevice-network.com/comment/bringing-internet-things-healthcare/ (archived at perma.cc/7KE3-LHEN)

10 McLaughlin, M (2018) How Data Analytics in Sports is Revolutionizing the Game, Biztechmagazine, 13 December. https://biztechmagazine.com/article/2018/12/how-data-analytics-revolutionizing-sports (archived at perma.cc/DLD3-B2WY)

11 Desjardins, J (2019) How Much Data is Generated Each Day? World Economic Forum, 17 April. Available from: https://www.weforum.org/agenda/2019/04/how-much-data-is-generated-each-day-cf4bddf29f/ (archived at perma.cc/R35K-JEUN)

12 Qlik (2018) *How to Drive Data Literacy in the Enterprise*, White paper. Available from: https://www.qlik.com/us/bi/-/media/08F37D711A58406E83B A8418EB1D58C9.ashx?ga-link=datlitreport_resource-library (archived at perma.cc/JDM4-89HN)

13 Desjardins, J (2019) How Much Data is Generated Each Day? World Economic Forum, 17 April. Available from: https://www.weforum.org/agenda/2019/04/how-much-data-is-generated-each-day-cf4bddf29f/ (archived at perma.cc/K8XR-3JNW)

14 Morris, T (2020) How Much Data by 2025? [Blog], Microstrategy, 6 January. Available from: https://www.microstrategy.cn/us/resources/blog/bi-trends/how-much-data-by-2025 (archived at perma.cc/D6JJ-BW23)

02

The four levels of analytics

Data and analytics – there are four levels?

Now that we have a knowledge of the world of data, an understanding of the holistic world of analytics is needed to ensure organizations and individuals can both capitalize on and utilize data and analytics effectively. Having a strong understanding of this world of analytics is a necessity and key to truly implementing a strong data and analytical strategy. Without understanding the different levels of analytics, organizations may buy software, source data, and democratize self-service tools, not knowing if those are the correct things they should be doing. The world of analytics is set on a premise of four levels of analytics: descriptive, diagnostic, predictive, and prescriptive. To understand the necessity of learning these levels of analytics, we need to take a step back and consider how organizations have viewed data and analytics historically. This picture will allow each of us to see how organizations should view data and analytics, and how organizations can use these four levels to drive success.

Now, let's begin: how have organizations viewed data and analytics historically? Historically speaking, organizations have spent a lot on investments in data and analytical technology, software, and tools. They have viewed the software and technology as the 'answers to their prayers', with answers that will drive all the data and analytic solutions. Organizations have been investing in technology that can help them realize their goals and 'data and analytical' dreams... yes, whether you want to believe it or not, data and analytical dreams are real things. Going back to the first release of Microsoft Excel (did you know it was first released for the Apple Macintosh, crazy right?) in 1985,[1] and any earlier software used for spreadsheets or analysis, organizations have either been buying or selling the software, thinking it would solve and do 'magical' things. As we know, this software is designed to store, use, and analyze data and information. As technology has expanded, evolved, and improved, so have investments in technology. In fact, it was predicted that worldwide revenues for big data and business analytics would be $187 billion in 2019.[2] That market is not slowing down... but there has been an unfortunate trend with this number and adoption of these products. With the large data literacy skills gap at 24 per cent of business decision-makers and 32 per cent of executives, investments in data and analytic technology are not succeeding the way they should. In fact, the large data literacy skills gap that was spoken of in Chapter 1, with only 24 per cent of business decision-makers and 32 per cent of executives confident in their data literacy skills, impairs these investments from taking off.

So, then, how does an understanding of the four levels of analytics impact this adoption and return on investment for all the money being invested into data and analytics? When organizations and individuals understand the four levels of analytics, it allows them to understand how an organization's workforce, individual talent and skills, plus technical prowess, can work together to build the organization's data and analytical strategy correctly. This will then allow the workforce to implement that strategy.

The four levels of analytics

Now, after that brief history lesson, let's start by understanding the four levels of analytics themselves. Then, with that understanding, we will show how different skill levels in the organization, from entry level employees all the way to executives, can use these four levels to 1) drive data and analytical strategy, 2) make smarter, data informed decisions, and 3) make the correct 'puzzle' view of data and analytics. In the end, an understanding of the four levels of analytics allows the

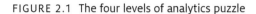

FIGURE 2.1 The four levels of analytics puzzle

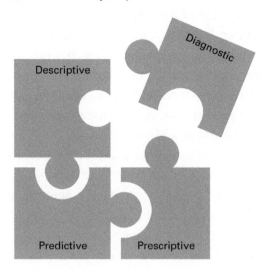

organization to not shoot blindly at the target, but really work towards a strong and powerful vision and strategy.

As was mentioned before, the four levels of analytics are descriptive, diagnostic, predictive, and prescriptive (Figure 2.1). To help us develop a sound foundational knowledge of each level, we will now define and provide examples of each of these levels of analytics. Along with definitions and examples, we will share specific software and technology that helps in that specific level. Then, once we have a sound and strong understanding of each level, we will look to how these different levels work together to formulate the right analytical picture and can truly help an organization succeed with their data investments.

First, before we jump into the first level, let's get a good grip on what the word analytics actually means. Analytics is a word we hear all the time, but do we really know what it means?

If we look up the definition of the word 'analytics', it means 'the systematic computational analysis of data or statistics'.[3]

What in the world does that mean? Analysis, when you google it, means the detailed examination of the elements or structure of something. In the world of data and analytics, analysis is the ability to dig into the data and information and understand what they say. The word 'information' is key here, as data is not always numbers, but can be symbols, words, and other elements If we understand what the data and information say, we can then also look at what are the elements and structure of the data and information, and so much more. This power of analytics and understanding it allows us to make better decisions, ask better questions, and fully empower ourselves with data.

The four levels of analytics – descriptive, diagnostic, predictive, and prescriptive – allow organizations to truly understand the data and information that their company builds, stores, and utilizes. When the organization understands the data and information, it can be utilized for business decisions, improvement, and success. Understanding and, better yet, implementing the four levels of analytics is crucial and essential for organizations to thrive in the current digital and data driven world.

Level 1: Descriptive analytics

The first level of analytics is descriptive analytics.

> If we were to go in and look for the definition of the word 'descriptive', we use our friend Google and discover it means 'serving or seeking to describe'. Then, of course we have to look up the definition of describe: 'Give an account in words (of someone or something), including all the relevant characteristics, qualities, or events.'

Well, what does that mean? Descriptive in this case means to describe something that has happened. In other words, with descriptive analytics we are looking back at something that has happened in the business, using data and analytics to make it happen.

That doesn't necessarily give us the clearest picture though. To help with this, there are other words out there that help define and paint the picture of descriptive analytics: reporting, dashboards, or observations. These are words we are probably all more familiar with. How often in a meeting or email are we hearing the word 'report'? How often do we see dashboards, KPIs, and so forth? These words are now so commonplace that they roll right off the tongue and are key to truly understanding descriptive analytics. Descriptive analytics is the building of reports, dashboards, and observations that help an organization know what has happened to that organization in the past, or what is currently happening.

With an understanding of descriptive analytics, we can understand and learn the role it plays in the data and analytical strategy puzzle. But, will understanding descriptive analytics automatically help organizations build their data and analytical puzzle? There is a key element to understand here: descriptive analytics poses a large struggle and challenge for organizations. One might ask, why? Descriptive analytics poses a unique challenge that the other levels of analytics do not: descriptive analytics can cause organizations to not move past the first level of analytics, hindering their growth and success with data.

With the four levels of analytics, organizations need to ensure they are not 'stuck' in a level or spending too much time in the designated level of analytics. With a large skills gap in the world of data and analytics, people who are asked to use data through the democratization of data will gravitate to the easiest form of analytics they are capable of. In most cases, that means descriptive analytics, as to look at a chart or dashboard, one can see what has happened and do ok in reading the information. In the case of organizations being stuck in a level, organizations around the world spend the majority of their time in descriptive analytics.

This happens because descriptive analytics are a comfortable thing, if one thinks about it. All of us have the ability to look backwards and describe things: what did we do last weekend? Did you like the movie you went and saw (and if it is a Star Wars movie, everyone had better say yes)? Or, in the case of businesses, what does this dashboard show us? What happened in the marketing campaign? How many employees did we hire last quarter? And so forth. Along with this, descriptive analytics and looking back lends to the curiosity of what has happened in the past to the organization.

Because of this comfort with descriptive analytics, combined with a lack of data skills, most employees in a given workforce are stuck in level 1, not knowing how to use data to make smarter decisions. In reality, a lot of employees do not even know there are four levels of analytics. With this lack of understanding, organizations are spending a lot of money on software and pretty data visualizations, but aren't really moving the needle with smart, data informed decisions. Therefore, finding themselves stuck in level 1 is a way organizations expand their own skills gap.

Now, a little side note for us: organizations should not work for an equal weighting between the four levels of analytics. This means organizations should not have their workforce spending 25 per cent of analytical muscle in each of the four levels; it is weighed unequally through the four levels. As organizations work to develop and employ true analytical solutions, they will find themselves dividing out the time between the four levels of analytics and the workforce. We will see that although descriptive analytics is important, most time in the organization should be spent in the second level of analytics, but more on that in a little.

One main reason descriptive analytics is so prevalent is the lack of data literacy skills that exist in the world. If one thinks about it, if you do not have a good understanding of how to use data, then how are you going to be good at the four levels of analytics?

Finally, there is a massive prevalence of data visualization in the world. Now, data visualization is necessary and vital to the success of an organization succeeding with data and analytics. Data viz, as it is sometimes known, simplifies and makes data and analytics easier for people to utilize, but data visualization is not the be-all and end-all in data and analytics. A data visualization, or dashboard, is great for summarizing or describing what has gone on in the past, but if people don't know how to progress beyond looking just backwards on what has happened, then they cannot diagnose and find the 'why' behind it.

As organizations invest in business intelligence tools, there is a prevalence of building dashboards for dashboards' sake and making a visualization as beautiful as possible. This can be detrimental for organizations that want to really emphasize the power of full data and analytics. I agree that data visualizations should be visually appealing, driving and utilizing the appeal and power for individuals to utilize it effectively, but sometimes this can take too much time, taking it away from more valuable uses in data. Plus, if the data visualization is not moving the needle of a business goal or objective, how effective is that visualization?

To help us develop a stronger understanding of the first level of analytics, understanding the types of software and technology that lend themselves to descriptive analytics can help. The technology is not earth-shattering, and most people have heard of the things about to be mentioned. How many of us have heard the term 'business intelligence' software, or BI for short? There are many different BI tools available today: Microsoft Power BI, Tableau, Qlik, ThoughtSpot, and so forth. All these are great tools that really lend themselves to descriptive analytics, and, yes, they do have some capability to drive in the other levels of analytics, but their real purpose is for descriptive analytics. Organizations should be making investments in these types of software and technology.

The first level of analytics is vital. We must know what happened in the past, so we can diagnose, build predictions, and so forth in the data. But it is only the first step of the process, not the full process itself. Utilizing knowledge of the first level of analytics helps to drive a better understanding of the second level.

Level 2: Diagnostic analytics

OK, now that we have wrapped our heads round level 1, level 2 should becomes easier to understand. To start, how about an analogy? Imagine you are sick and have been sick for a few days. You have run a fever, chills, have a cough, and, well, look sick. You set up an appointment to visit your doctor to get help. You wait in the doctor's office and they finally walk in. They look you up and down, check your vitals, and then say to you, 'Yep, you are sick', only to then walk out and never return. How satisfied would you be with that doctor? Did that doctor help you? Better yet, would you ever see that doctor again? All the doctor did was tell you what you already know. Guess what? That is *descriptive* analytics. The doctor was able to describe your symptoms and that you were sick, but they didn't do anything to help you.

Now, imagine the doctor looks at you and checks your vitals, describes the illness's symptoms, then asks you questions to get to the root of the problem and works to properly diagnose your illness. With this diagnosis, the doctor has the ability to help you to overcome and improve your situation. This is the second level of analytics, *diagnostic*.

Now that we have painted a hopefully good picture of how the first level can lead to the second level, let's dig into the root of the word diagnose or diagnostic.

If we use our friendly little Google once more, the definition of 'diagnose' is 'identify the nature of (an illness or other problem) by examination of the symptoms'.

OK, in the world of data and analytics, we aren't diagnosing the illnesses of people or animals, but we are diagnosing what is happening in the business and getting to the root of things and understanding why something is happening. Another strong term to use with diagnostic analytics is insight: diagnostic analytics is getting the insight in the data, learning the drivers and why things happened. The second level of analytics is essential to succeeding with data and analytical strategies. Why is this?

To understand the importance of the second level of analytics, we need to understand the purpose of using data and analytics in general. Why do organizations utilize data and analytics? Why do organizations spend not just thousands but millions of dollars to source, utilize, and analyze data and information? The answers are ones we are all familiar with. The world is now digital, the use of data and analytics is now non-negotiable, and organizations need to capitalize on data. However, what happens when those utilizing the data do not know how to get insight from said data? What if they are not comfortable 'diagnosing' what is going on in the data, similar to the doctor who could only tell you that you were sick. By empowering a workforce to get to the root of problems through diagnostic analytics, the organization has a greater chance to succeed with the data and analytic investments they are making.

Another key element to understand within the second level of analytics, and the first level for that matter, is the democratization of data that organizations are using to get data to the masses. First, what does it mean to democratize anything? It means to put things in the hands of the masses, giving power and freedom for a workforce to utilize the information presented to them. A workforce is made up of people with many different backgrounds and experiences, and these unique abilities should help organizations succeed with data in a smarter, more effective manner.

As with the first level of analytics, there are many tools and software applications in the world today that are designed to help an organization succeed with diagnostic analytics. Some of these vendors are the exact same as those in the descriptive analytics world: Microsoft Excel, Microsoft Power BI, Qlik and Tableau. Through this democratization of data, organizations look to empower individuals to not only describe what is happening in the data, but also to find the insight to why it is happening.

The key word is insight, which at the second level could be called the insight level and allows us to merge how the first and second level work together. When one looks at the first level of analytics, it is describing *what* has happened, and this leads to the second level of analytics, which is exploring *why* that thing happened. Here we can see how the second level truly should be where the majority of a workforce spends most their time in the world of data and analytics. As dashboards, reports, and observations are made in the first level, the workforce can use their data literacy skills to figure out why the observations are saying what they do. For example, why did the trend line vary so much against prior quarters? Why did we see a shift in the demographic bar chart? And so forth.

Along with this merging of levels 1 and 2, all organizations need to make smarter decisions with data (and us as individuals for that matter… have you seen the world today?). This is the essence of the first two levels. Individuals and organizations should be using data and analytics to be more data informed. By being data informed, individuals are now using descriptive analytics to see what has or is happening, then diagnosing it to understand why, and can use that information to make a smart data-informed decision. More on data informed decision-making in a later chapter. As organizations start to truly mature in their abilities to use the first two levels of analytics effectively, they will start to see data and analytical strategy success.

Level 3: Predictive analytics

When you think of the word 'prediction', what comes to your mind? Is it the great Nostradamus who predicted, well, it seems everything? Is it predictions of who is going to win the big game or when a flight is going to land? Or is it the prediction of what the weather is going to be the next week as you leave on that big vacation you are eagerly anticipating? There are many things that we look to predict in our lives and careers. As we do so, of course we would like to strike the golden ticket and become excellent at building predictions in all areas of our lives, and the same can be said for organizations looking to capitalize on data and analytics.

First, we can bring back the doctor analogy to understand a continuous step within the world of analytics. As we remember our doctor came in and said that we were sick, but then left for the foreseeable future, not really helping us at all (I mean, we could tell we were sick, right?). Then, our doctor took the next step, and was able to diagnose the 'why' behind our illness, helping us to understand what was going on to cause the illness, leading us to consider ways to overcome the illness. Now, once we know the 'why', what does a doctor usually do? They look to prescribe things that will help us to get better; in essence, the doctor is making a prediction that if we do 'A' then 'B' will follow.

Let's dive into a deeper understanding of the third level of analytics by look at the definition of the word 'prediction' or 'predict'.

If we turn to our friend Google again (we are using this imaginary friend of Google a lot, aren't we?), we will find that the definition of the word predict is 'say or estimate that (a specified thing) will happen in the future or will be a consequence of something'.

I really love the definition of the word 'predict'. First, we say or estimate that something will happen in the future. Let's digest this part of the definition. With predictions, we say it will happen or we take the time to estimate something that will happen. That sounds great, but the second part of the definition is where I like to focus my attention – on the word 'predict', especially when it comes to organizations who are looking to utilize data and analytics to their advantage.

The second part of the definition says 'or will be a consequence of something'. How often do we look to do something in business because we feel it will have the desired outcome we want? This is a constant thing in our careers: someone says, 'If we do this, that will happen.' Unfortunately, as we know all too well, that doesn't always happen. Now, if we combine it with the power of data and analytics, the power of the third level of analytics, maybe we can make those predictions and consequences happen more often.

Predictive analytics is one of the most popular forms of analytics we hear about in the world today, and it has become almost synonymous with data science and strategy. Why has predictive analytics become so popular? See if these terms are familiar to you: data science, statistics, machine learning, algorithm, big data, and so forth. These are the terms that make up the third, and part of the fourth, level of analytics. The commonality of these terms in our day and age has led to a problem with the roll-out of data and analytical investments in general.

With the advent of these words, and as they have expanded across the globe, individuals and organizations have been over-hyping the power of these tools and skills. It is like the big game coming up and only having it be a massive let down. Now, don't get me wrong, the abilities of predictive analytics are very powerful, but without a data literate workforce, it becomes very difficult to utilize the world of predictive analytics appropriately. Let's jump into this with an example.

Imagine to yourself you are a statistician who has built a strong predictive model on the upcoming holiday season shopping schedule. In this model, you were able to source the correct data (which can be hard at times, we know) that helped drive a smart decision. Through the model, you build a presentation and start to share the message around. Unfortunately, as you start to talk about your analysis and share the results, the people you are speaking to are looking at you with blank stares. You get frustrated as you share more and more, as very few are accepting and understanding the message. You start to wonder why no one is getting the message? The big issue does not lie in your model, analysis, or the technology; the problem lies within the data culture that exists in the organization and the lack of data skills.

As organizations have invested dollar after dollar in predictive analytics teams, data science, and technology, it seems the less they are able to capitalize on these investments. With the organization not able to absorb data and analytics, it subsequently renders the predictive modeling and analytics potentially useless. With a stronger skill set within the workforce, predictive analytics can succeed.

What technologies and software are utilized to help bring success to predictive analytics? There are many types of software and technologies available for organizations to use and succeed with our third level of analytics. First, there are two main languages that are gaining more and more popularity for data science and predictive analytics: Python and R. These are very, very popular coding languages that allow statisticians, quants, data scientists, and more to build out modeling. Plus, who doesn't want to code using languages called Python and R? One is the name of a snake and the other, if you drag it out, makes you sound like a pirate.

Along with the coding languages, there are software companies in existence that allow us to simplify data science and make it easier for end users, those more comfortable with the first two levels of analytics. The reality is, the majority of a workforce doesn't need to be data scientists, they just need comfort with data literacy. Examples of these software companies are Alteryx, SAS, Apache Spark, D3, and more. One can even use Microsoft Excel, Tableau, and Qlik to drive predictive analytics.

The types of employees that help to drive predictive analytics have already been mentioned: data scientists, statisticians, quants, and so forth. Even data analysts can drive predictive analytics. Plus, with the world of data literacy being as big as it is, and with the non-technical people now having a large place at the data and analytical table, everyone who can speak and use the language of data can be a part of predictive analytics. Therefore, when a model, analysis, and the like are completed, those who are working mainly in the worlds of descriptive and diagnostic analytics can participate through understanding and discussing the predictive level of analytics.

Level 4: Prescriptive analytics

Now we have reached the last level of analytics: prescriptive analytics. When we speak of the term prescriptive analytics, there are different definitions and interpretations. For our purposes, we speak of the data and technology itself prescribing what should be done with the data and analytics, and what business decision should be made. In this case, the data and technology itself prescribes or advises on what should be done. This level of analytics is quite advanced, but doesn't necessarily need many people to run; it just needs a lot of people who can interpret and utilize the information to make smarter, informed decisions.

When we look at the world of prescriptive analytics, we need to look at it from a way to augment the human element. Technology utilized for prescriptive analytics has the ability to dissect and sift through massive quantities of data, allowing us to speed up the analytical process and eliminate the potential for human error, but we must then be able to utilize the data and information presented to us. Prescriptive analytics has the great ability to build for us a strong analytical outcome, but it is up to the human side of data to make informed decisions with it.

What kinds of technologies go into the world of prescriptive analytics? There are many different applications available, from a more self-service perspective with Domo or Alteryx, to more advanced technologies like SAS or SAP Predictive Analytics. These tools are a great way to help with your world of prescriptive analytics, but without a workforce that knows how to utilize data and information (analytics) to make smart, data informed decisions for businesses, then the investment could really be wasted, and no return be found.

Real-world examples of the four levels of analytics

To help us build out a broader foundation and knowledge of the four levels of analytics, understanding real-world examples of each level of analytics helps to paint the appropriate picture. To help drive the foundation even deeper, each level will build upon the previous level, giving us an overall picture of how the four levels work together. Overall, this is a fantastic way to help us also find where different roles and individuals play a part in the analytical system.

Level 1: Descriptive analytics

Each one of these examples can be drawn to other real-world examples. Descriptive analytics is a common part of the business world and each one of us is presented with descriptive analytics on a regular basis:

- the monthly revenue dashboard presented to the enterprises sales leader;
- the quarterly marketing report on click-through rates;
- the organization's quarterly net promoter score report.

What roles play a part with descriptive analytics? Every one! The c-suite executive group, with reading dashboards, business and data analysts building the dashboards and reports, data scientists using descriptive analytics to describe the technical analysis that was performed, end users reading and interpreting dashboards, and so forth. Everyone plays a strong part with descriptive analytics.

Level 2: Diagnostic analytics

Remember, each example of descriptive analytics is the first step of the analytical landscape. It represents what has happened in the past and diagnostic analytics shows us why it happened.

- Within the monthly revenue dashboard, the sales leader saw a nice increase in sales quarter-over-quarter and wondered 'why' it happened. A data analyst went through, analyzed the information, spoke to the sales reps, and found a new incentive program helped drive more revenue from the field reps.

- In the quarterly marketing report on click-through rates, marketing noticed a sharp decline in click-through rates. In the past 12 months, the first seven months saw a consistent rate, and then in month eight a sharp decline took place and that same rate has continued. The chief marketing officer wants to know 'why' that decline took place. Through the analysis, it was found out the marketing team moved the location of the click-through link to a new location in the email. Through this, it was discovered it was harder to see and a change was made for future email advertising.

- In the organization's quarterly net promoter score, rates held steady except for one: 'Would you recommend our company to a friend?' This score rose in a strong fashion, and the team analyzed the data, to that find a glitch in the system made it appear that the net promoter score rose well. By finding this glitch, the organization saved money and prevented a promotion of what was found to be a false positive in the data.

What roles play a part with diagnostic analytics? Every one! Those who want things to be diagnosed, like the c-suite and decision-makers, ask the questions of the diagnostic analytics. Data analysts work to dig into the information around the descriptive dashboard and report.

Data scientist can run models to figure out what is happening. Those who work in different business units in the company can provide their expertise and insight into procedures, recent launches, and so forth. Overall, everyone can play a part to help diagnose why something has happened.

Level 3: Predictive analytics

Predictive analytics takes us into a more advanced level of analytics. Predictive analytics takes us into what 'will' happen.

- The sales team want to ensure they capitalize on the new momentum gathered from the incentive-based rise in revenue. The data science team are looking to build new models that allow the field reps to see exactly what went well with the sales and revenue side, helping them to predict 'If the reps do this, this will happen.' Doing so can help project and continue the momentum.
- The marketing team looked at the data and information, using its analysts, and worked to run projections on changes to the link. They ran multiple tests that allow them to build predictions for a launch of the new email campaigns and where to place the link. Through the analysis, the marketing team now have a full report of predictions.
- After finding the glitch, the team went back to looking for ways to enhance the promoter score, utilizing the powerful data sourcing and technology they have, building predictive models to analyze and improve the company's score.

What roles play a part with predictive analytics? Every one! Of course, data science and more technical roles matter a lot, as they will build predictions and models. When the c-suite want to predict what will happen with certain actions, they must communicate that well with the team building the predictions. Different business units need to communicate plans, history, experience, and so forth, so teams can build proper predictions.

Level 4: Prescriptive analytics

Prescriptive analytics is where the technology itself is telling the organization what to do.

- The sales team can now allow the massive data being gained through the incentive-based approach and utilize machine learning to find trends, patterns, and let the machine tell the teams what they should be doing. It is crucial the team can ask strong questions of the data and then also implement the right answers.

- The marketing group can now allow the massive data being sourced and produced from the click-through rates and email campaigns to utilize algorithms and the technology to advise on new placements of links.

- With net promoter score, the real work is not analyzing the data, but in the work, service, and more that goes into the organization. The c-suite work with the data team to allow the machines to find patterns and prescribe what things can be done to see success. Maybe it is an extra phone call or slight bump in return for customers, whatever the case may be. This allows the company to test and succeed with net promoter score.

What roles play a part with prescriptive analytics? Every one! Again, like predictive analytics, the technical matters a lot, but we need everyone with the strong ability to ask questions of the machines and then to implement the work and analysis the machine gives us.

Chapter summary

When we look at the four levels of analytics and the world it occupies, there is a strong current for all of us to understand what underlies each level. The current occupies the flow and work that should be seen throughout a strong analytical puzzle, and who doesn't get satisfaction when a puzzle is completed? For the organization to succeed with data and analytics, the puzzle needs to be put together correctly.

We can't put the puzzle together like a little child who tries to fit each piece together. Investment needs to be made throughout each level, a proper undertaking that involves both the investment in the human element and capabilities, plus the software and technology element.

We have seen that descriptive analytics is describing what happened in the past, diagnostic analytics is finding out why something happened, predictive analytics is predicting the future, and prescriptive analytics is allowing the machines to help us know what we should do. With this understanding in place, organizations can fully develop and succeed with a strong data and analytical strategy. Along with this understanding, who is ready to learn the definition of the term 'data literacy'? Jump into the next chapter to find out more.

Notes

1 CIS Poly (undated) History of Microsoft Excel. Available from: http://cis.poly. edu/~mleung/CS394/f06/week01/Excel_history.html (archived at https://perma. cc/48W2-BZWF)

2 Olavsrud, T (2016) Big Data and Analytics Spending to hit $187 Billion, CIO, 24 May. Available from: https://www.cio.com/article/3074238/big-data-and-analytics-spending-to-hit-187-billion.html (archived at https://perma.cc/ U6W2-5P39)

3 Google definitions (2020) Definition of Analytics. Available from: https:// www.google.com/search?q=definition+of+analytics&rlz=1C1GCEB_enUS858U S858&oq=definition+of+analytics&aqs=chrome..69i57j69i59j69i60l4j69i61j69 i60.2410j0j4&sourceid=chrome&ie=UTF-8 (archived at https://perma.cc/ N2AQ-4LQ5)

03

Defining data literacy

Now that we have an understanding that our world is consumed by data, and we understand the four levels of analytics, should we *finally* define just what in the world data literacy is? Yes, so let's do this!

In order to define what data literacy is, we first need to understand what it is not: data literacy is not data science. Not everyone in the world needs to be a data scientist, but everyone needs to be data literate. I know everyone was expecting that they would have to go back to school, learn the technical aspects of data, statistics, and so forth. In fact, that is not the case (and everyone rejoiced, saying thank you to Jordan!).

Data scientists are advanced in their technical skills. They like to do coding, statistics, and so forth. In its purest form, data science is where an individual uses the scientific method on data. That's right, we are all going back to our younger education days to remember the scientific method. How many of you want to go back to that world? I am guessing not many of us. Again, not everyone needs to take that path, but we do need to get everyone learning, utilizing, and succeeding with data. Not only will this allow all of us to compete and future-proof our careers to the future economy, but it gives everyone practical skills that will also benefit our lives.

With our analysis of data science out of the way, let's get down to the business of the definition of data literacy. It is easy to find different definitions on data literacy, but we will focus in on an all-encompassing definition that was solidified by Emerson University and MIT. It is:

The ability to read, work with, analyze, and argue with data.[1]

I really like this definition, but I want to expand and modify the 'argue with' characteristic to bring us more clarity. The last phrase 'argue with' can be a little vague, and in this case, it means to support your argument with data. Yes, this is vital, but let's give that characteristic a little more meat on the bones. We will evolve the definition to be: data literacy is the ability to read, work with, analyze, and *communicate* with data. This small shift in the definition allows us to expand our arguing, as communicating data doesn't always mean we will be arguing. The ability to communicate with data isn't only about supporting one's argument utilizing the backing of data, although that is an important part. The ability to back up our 'gut feel' with data really enhances our value to our companies. Another aspect of communicating with data can be storytelling with data, which brings context and applicability to the analysis and statistics performed.

Now that we have the definition in place, we are all set to march forward with data literacy and to succeed in the future economy, right? End of book! If it were that easy, then we would all be ready and set with data literacy, and this book wouldn't need to exist. The reality is, though, we also need this book to expand, elaborate, and extend our knowledge to new levels when it comes to data literacy. To do this, let's jump into each separate part and characteristic in the definition of data literacy, allowing us to expand our knowledge. To help us, we will use examples of the four characteristics of data literacy throughout our study, empowering us to know real-world examples of where these skills are needed.

Characteristic 1: Reading data

The first characteristic in the meaning of data literacy is reading data. Well, what does it mean to read data? What does it mean to read anything? Providing real-world examples and defining the word will allows us to start growing our understanding. When we open up the figurative Oxford Dictionary (online now, of course), we find the definition of the word 'read' is: 'look at and comprehend the meaning of (written or printed matter) by mentally interpreting the characters or symbols of which it is composed'.[2] Huh? That sounds pretty complicated for the word 'read'. I mean, we are all familiar with that word, you are reading this book right now. In our case, let's expand the definition a little bit. In the Oxford definition, it mentions written or printed matter, but what about reading body language? Can't one get a lot of information from reading a person's body language or attitude? I think we can absolutely read and learn from body language. But 'read' also means to look at something and comprehend it. To me, that is the most important meaning we can draw with data literacy: to look at some data and information, comprehending it. Can we expand on this further? Can we expand the data literacy characteristic of reading data to add more value? Why don't we jump in and find out.

In our case, to read data means to look at the data and information presented and comprehend it. Plain and simple. In the world of data, there are many forms that data comes in and will be presented, shown to each and every one of us. Reading data is our ability to look at and comprehend the data and information, when we possess it, which empowers us to succeed with data. Herein lies one of the strong reasons why there is a large skills gap and why organizations are stuck at the first level of analytics: people are basic in their skills to read and comprehend data as it is presented to them. When people are only comfortable reading in the first level of analytics, descriptive analytics, their comfort will have them going back to the first level on an ongoing basis. This is something we all do. Maybe it is our evolution. We all revert to where we are comfortable (this is why closing the skills gap is so important: making everyone comfortable with data literacy). Picture finding your most favourite spot on a couch and never wanting to leave it. If we aren't comfortable with reading deeper into the data and analytics presented to us, we will choose to stick to the first level of analytics, aka our favourite spot.

With the knowledge that reading data means the ability to look at and comprehend the data presented to us, it will help us to understand that not everyone will read data with the same skills and abilities. Nor does everyone *need* to read the same level: think of the chain of command. Executives have one level, vice presidents and decision-makers probably another, all the way throughout an organization to data scientists. With the overall skill, the ability to interpret a data visualization and bring our own personal flare to it can really open up and enhance our skills with all four levels of analytics. To help us understand the varying skills, let's tie it to a potential real-world example and use this to expand our mind with how different roles will need to read data and information differently.

Let's imagine we work in a large retail organization that is excited about a recent product launch. This product launch has taken months to build, utilizing the strength of data literacy and analytics to guide a data informed decision. How did the different groups arrive at the decisions they did? Who had to 'read' the data to help in the process?

THE RESEARCH AND DEVELOPMENT TEAM VS READING DATA

First, let's look at the research and development team. They will need to read, understand, and utilize volumes worth of data and information to make a decision. In our case, the research and development team have invested time and energy in gathering internal and external data, and as a result the team have utilized the power of surveys, studied competitive and market intelligence to understand the viability of a new product, and so forth. As you can imagine, the team have used both descriptive and diagnostic analytics to read the data and find observations and insight leading to decisions that can be made

---

MARKETING GROUP VS READING DATA

Second, let's look at the marketing group, who are tasked with building marketing and messaging for the new product. The marketing group needs to look at and comprehend mountains of the organization's own data, plus study external trends for the product. What types of campaigns have worked in the past and what haven't? What external circumstances could influence the product launch? The ability to use both descriptive and diagnostic analytics help the marketing group to understand what type of marketing should be done to help the new product launch correctly and to succeed.

EXECUTIVE GROUP VS READING DATA

Third, let's look at the executive group, which pulls the ultimate lever on a product launch decision. The executive suite had better be able to read data to help make big decisions, like new product launches. Now, we know executive suites don't have a lot of free time on their hands, and they will probably spend a lot of their data literacy time reading data. Executives need the ability to read and quickly assess the data presented to them to make smart decisions. In this case, the executive team was able to read and digest quick information on the new product to make a smart, data informed decision.

Overall, as one can see, *everyone* has a need to read data in the organization. Each member of the organization has their own unique perspective. When one speaks of the ability to read data, it helps the entire organization to understand how to speak the language of data, which we will cover later. The ability to look at and comprehend has been vital in their decision-making approach.

Characteristic 2: Working with data

Sometimes, when we think of the word 'work', we may tell ourselves it is a bad word, but the reality is work should be as fun as play. Work is meant to be enjoyed and allow us to succeed with the life we want. In the world of data literacy, working with data should be a joy and not a burden; it should enhance our careers and help us move forward.

What does it mean to work with data or just work in general? Understanding the meaning of the word work will put it in better context and light.

When we look to the meaning of the word work, we can find many variations and ideas. I want to look at it as an 'activity involving mental or physical effort done in order to achieve a purpose or result'.[3] OK, so working with data is an activity with data that involves mental or physical effort done in order to achieve a purpose or result. Done, chapter over, we get it... right? OK, maybe not; let's dive into this further and understand it more.

Mark Twain is quoted as saying 'Work and play are words used to describe the same thing under differing conditions.'[4] Work is an activity that can be enjoyed. Now that we have a sound understanding of the word work and understand that work and play can be similar, diving into it within the world of data literacy and organizational work is helpful.

Again, we see that working with data is doing something with data in an organization to achieve a result or purpose. To help us understand working with data, tying working with data to the four levels of analytics will help us bring it to real-world context. Then, a nice flow through different parts of an organization looking at different roles within an organization helps us understand what they do working with data.

The four levels of analytics have a lot in common with working with data, as each level has unique and different ways to work with data. In the world of descriptive analytics, working with data can mean many different things to many different people and parts of the organization. Remember, descriptive analytics is the world of describing what has happened, or is currently happening, for an organization. When we utilize this characteristic of working with data, describing what has happened in the past is the exact definition of what we are looking for. Within the organization, whether you are the one building a data visualization on the latest marketing campaign or the one reading the developed data visualization, you are working with data; we are all working with data on a consistent basis. Think of our example from a previous chapter of Rolls-Royce and airplane engines. How many different ways are people working with data on those airplane engines alone? You have those building the sensors for data, those collecting data, and those analyzing the data to make it work for them. All of these people are *working with* data.

The second level of analytics, the world of diagnostic analytics, or finding the 'why' behind descriptive analytics, is again, littered with working with data. As one tries to diagnose the 'why' behind things, finding the insight, they are working with data. Whether it is asking questions, receiving a report or dashboard, driving analysis, you are working with data. Can you think of areas where you are looking for insight? Is it in watching your favorite sports team? In diagnosing what outfits to pack for a vacation? There are numerous ways *you* are already working with data. In our organizational example, think again on Rolls-Royce and airplane engines: what is the purpose of collecting all that information if we aren't going to work with it to find insight? Those working with data from the airplane engines have a great responsibility to find insight, especially if they are dealing with issues that can potentially save lives.

Predictive and prescriptive analytics *work with* data in many ways, from the different groups helping to build the sourcing of data, to the data scientists working with the data to build predictions and analysis, to the end group reading the data. Working with data is very common for you and for me; in fact, we do it all the time in our personal lives.

As was mentioned before, how often are we looking at trends in sports to try and decipher how our team are going to do in the big game against our rival? And so forth? *All... the... time!* We are constantly working with, and reading, data to empower our lives, but how does it look in the work setting? Let's do this and use another example.

In our next example, let's imagine we work in a large organization that is studying to launch a new and innovative marketing campaign; one the company has never done before. This campaign has taken months to build and study, and really goes against what the company has done in the past; many in the organization are nervous about this particular campaign. How do people work with data in this campaign? What would they be trying to discover and find? How does data literacy play a part? Let's study different groups and how they work with data to help launch and analyze the success of the campaign.

INFORMATION TECHNOLOGY TEAM VS WORKING WITH DATA

First off, let's look at the information technology team. Do they need to work with data to help launch a campaign like this? Of course they need to work with data. The information technology team for this particular campaign are assigned to source and make available the data needed to make smart, data informed decisions. The information technology team works with data in many, many ways. In doing so, the information technology team allow the end users to analyze and consume the data to help the campaign succeed.

MARKETING TEAM VS WORKING WITH DATA

Second off, let's look at the marketing team itself. Do they need to work with data to help launch a campaign like this? *Yes.* The marketing team should be working with data to look at, or build, the descriptive analytics. They should work with data to diagnose trends, patterns, and occurrences in the internal and external data. They should work with data to build predictions on how the campaign will succeed, so they can too.

SALES TEAM VS WORKING WITH DATA

Third, let's look at the sales team. The sales team is on the front line with customers and potential customers alike. The sales team is answering questions and inquiries on the campaign, the new products, what is available to your organizations' customers, and how they can utilize things for success. The sales reps should be well versed and educated on the data and information that went into building the marketing campaign, and have the information shared with them to help them with requests.

> **EXECUTIVE GROUP VS WORKING WITH DATA**
>
> Fourth, and finally, let's look at the executive group. The executive group had better be working with data to launch a new campaign, especially since it is out of their wheelhouse of comfort and what has been done historically. The executives will receive reports, dashboards, and data and information to help them make a data informed decision (look, see, the four levels of analytics coming together in our puzzle). As they receive this information, they are working with data. Yes, of course, the executive team needs to work with data to succeed here.

Overall, as one can see, *everyone* has a need to work with data in the organization and the ability to work with data has been vital in *everyone's* decision-making processes. Work, unfortunately, far too often has a negative connotation added to it, especially when it comes to data and analytics. Often, work is seen as statistics, coding, and so forth. Work should be like play, as Mark Twain has said. Data literacy type work should be done to help organizations succeed, to achieve goals and visions, and, as I like to say, make the needle move for a business. As people enhance data literacy skills and learn to work with data (again, we all work with data more than we may care to admit or may know), and do so with a happy spirit, they will find that working with data allows them to make smarter decisions. This ability to make smarter decisions is truly beneficial to not only our career, but also our lives in general. Who hasn't wanted the ability to make a better decision in choosing a career, buying a car or home, choosing fitness goals, and so forth? Working with data can help us to not feel overwhelmed by the data and technology, but to succeed with and use it to harness energy for our own good. Working with data needs to become synonymous with how we do our everyday jobs.

Characteristic 3: Analyzing data

Whoa, what in the world does it mean to analyze data? Isn't that only for the technical at heart or technically skilled? To analyze, doesn't one need to code? The answer to these questions is a resounding 'No!' Each of us possesses the ability to analyze data for good, to help us make smarter decisions, and to utilize data for our good and not for bad. Analyzing data also gives us a way to decipher and sift through the massive amounts of data and information presented to us in our lives. Most of us have heard the phrase 'fake news'. The proper ability to ask questions and analyze data and information can help us decipher through the misinformation presented to us. Whether we are analyzing data for our careers or in that little channel we call social media, analyzing data is the key element to the second level of analytics: diagnostic analytics.

When we think of the word 'analyze', many things may pop into our minds. This time we are going to analyze (see what I did there?) the word analysis to start:

detailed examination of the elements or structure of something.[5]

Sounds a bit to me like we want to examine something to figure out the 'why' behind it. The why, or insight, behind things is the key to the characteristic of analyzing data. Another piece of the puzzle is to 'discover or reveal (something) through detailed examination'.[6] I really love the word 'reveal'. When we reveal something, we are bringing to light, or revealing, the insight to the descriptive analytic, into the data and information presented to us. The question now becomes, how do we analyze data and information? How do we ourselves, if we don't have a technical background, reveal insight from data and information? Let's find out!

It all starts with questions, and then some more questions, and then maybe a few more questions. We need to get better at asking questions. How often do we just take things at face value and say to ourselves: this is it, I have found the answer? In our careers, unfortunately, I think we are trained that way. We step into roles, are given procedures and policies to follow, and set off on our path. Unfortunately, that doesn't foster a lot of question asking. Let's look at a real-world application we use everyday to analyze data: 'What clothes should I wear today?'

When we are deciding what to wear for the coming day, how many of us haphazardly throw on whatever is near us and just hope it coincides with the weather outside? If you are doing this, I hope you live in the Caribbean somewhere, where it is warm 99 per cent of the time and you can just guess... but, even then, you may regret it when a large storm passes through. For us to make smart and informed decisions on what to wear, we take in and analyze quite a bit of information. First, I am guessing we jump into our smart phones and analyze the weather app, hoping the prediction is accurate. From there, we can look out the window of where we currently are and we can visually analyze the information presented to us. Finally, we can march ourselves outside and actually *feel* the weather. These are all examples of analyzing data even when your methods don't use technology and you are just making first-person observations.

Every one of us is analyzing data and information on a continual basis to make smart, data informed decisions. Thinking about how different business units would look at data with a product launch can help us understand this.

RESEARCH AND DEVELOPMENT TEAM VS ANALYZING DATA

First off, do the research and development team need to analyze data to understand how the new product launch performed? *Yes!* The research and development team will analyze not only internal information, the information coming from the company's data sourcing, but also external data. For example, you launch a product and at the same time the overall economy takes a bit of a dive into a recession. One can quickly say the launch failed and it was a bad idea, but was it really? If external data tells us that the economy as a whole struggled, maybe that is the driver of the negative launch. The research and development team will work hard to ask questions and analyze information to see if the product launch was successful.

PRODUCT TEAM VS ANALYZING DATA

Second, let's look at the product team itself. Does the product team need to analyze data to understand how successful the launch was? Yes, of course. The product team will ask many questions, study many factors, and analyze many pieces of data to understand how successful the launch was.

EXECUTIVE TEAM VS ANALYZING DATA

Third, and finally, let's go back and study our wonderful executive team again. Does the executive team need to analyze data to understand how successful the launch was? Yes, and I sure hope so! The executive team is running your company, and if they are not analyzing the success of product launches, I sure would like to know what they are doing... just shooting from the hip? Executives need to analyze a lot of information to understand success: how did it impact the bottom line, or did it? How many of the new products were built and how many sold? How well is the sales team selling the item?

How well is marketing creating enthusiasm about the product? So many questions, and this is just the tip of the iceberg. All of this is the third characteristic of data literacy: analyzing the data. Yes, of course the executive team needs the characteristic of analyzing data to successfully study the product launch. The ability to analyze data is vital in its understanding of product launch success.

Overall, as we can see, *everyone* also has a need to analyze data. The ability to analyze data is vital in its understanding of product launch success. Everyone needs the ability to find trends and patterns in the data and information. Everyone has a need to 'discover or reveal (something) through detailed examination', as our definition says. Not everyone needs to be a data scientist, but everyone needs to drive questions and analysis. Everyone needs to dig into the information to be successful with diagnostic analytics. This is one of the biggest keys of data literacy: analyzing data. Yes, all four characteristics are key to success with data and analytical strategies, but if we can't analyze the information for insight, we will continue the problem of being stuck at level 1: descriptive analytics.

Characteristic 4: Communicating with data

Now that we have covered reading, working with, and analyzing data, we now turn to a very important point about data literacy: communicating with data. What would we do if we built a strong analysis, found some great insight through diagnostic analytics, but possessed no skills to communicate it to the masses? Or, maybe worse yet, what if you thought you had skills to communicate and you clearly didn't; you clearly couldn't get the point across? Communicating with data is an absolute necessity.

For the last characteristic, understanding what communicating with data means is critical. The word communicate means:

share or exchange information, news, or ideas.[7]

In our case, thinking of the four levels of analytics, we are looking at sharing or exchanging information to describe what happened in the past; sharing news or an idea of great insight in diagnostic analytics; sharing the predictions being made in predictive and prescriptive analytics. The power to communicate is necessary to succeeding with data and analytical strategy. How should we communicate with data? Is there a special way we can communicate with data literacy that will make it more impactful? I am so glad you asked!

There is a growing field within the world of data and analytics: data storytelling. Why is this field growing quickly? Taking a moment to think through this will help. If I were to share many statistics and numbers in these chapters, how quickly would you tell your friends: 'I have the best book to read to help you get to sleep at night'? Now, let's take a look at a different scenario. How often do you remember the stories and thoughts shared by people? The reality is, our minds do better with stories than with data. We need to empower people to share stories and communicate the results, analyses, and insights found within the data.

Turning now towards our familiar way of looking at different business units and whether they need to use the data literacy characteristic, let us imagine we are studying our company's financial performance over the past 12 months. The last 12 months have been a very successful time for the company, so successful, in fact, that we want to know what is driving the success and can it be maintained. Do different business units in the company need to communicate what the data is telling them?

FINANCE TEAM VS COMMUNICATING WITH DATA

First, let's look at the finance team. Does the finance team need to communicate with data to understand how successful the past 12 months were? *Yes!* In fact, it is the finance team that needs to communicate the result. In this case, the finance team may only need to share the descriptive analytics, so level 1. The finance team will share the numbers and results with the executive team and the rest of the company. The finance team must effectively communicate the results to paint the right picture.

DATA SCIENCE VS COMMUNICATING WITH DATA

Second, let's look at the data science team. The data science team can play a very effective role in understanding what has truly happened over the last 12 months. The data science team can find, analyze, and uncover things that others may have missed. In fact, the characteristic of communicating with data is really where data scientists can strengthen their data literacy skills. The question could be asked: do data scientists have a need to learn more within data literacy? The answer is a resounding 'Yes!' Historically, communicating might not have been at the top of the list of desired skills with data scientists. But, in the new world of data, that must change, and data scientists must develop the skill to communicate with all audiences in the company.

↓

EXECUTIVE TEAM VS COMMUNICATING WITH DATA

Third, and finally, let's look at the executive team. The executive team needs to be able to communicate the results that were found in different analyses. They need to then communicate out and share what the drivers were and what kind of success was there, what they plan to do to keep the success going, and so forth.

The ability to communicate data is vital to the understandings of the company's success. Overall, we can see the common theme that runs throughout the world of data literacy: *everyone* needs the skill to communicate with data.

Chapter summary

As we have clearly seen through the chapter, everyone, and I mean everyone, needs to develop skills within data literacy. Remember, the definition of data literacy is the ability to read, work with, analyze, and communicate with data. Whether the company is launching a product, changing campaigns, and so forth, data literacy and its characteristics will help the organization succeed.

Two key points to conclude with are ones that should be overarching pieces of the definition of data literacy: data fluency and data informed decision-making. Now, this will be covered later in the book, but data fluency is how it sounds – the ability of people to speak the language of data. The second point, data informed decision-making, is making decisions with data. If we aren't making smarter decisions with data because of data literacy, then what's the point? Data literacy is to empower us all and it truly will, if we allow it.

Notes

1 Knight, M (2019) The Importance of Data Literacy, Dataversity.net, 12 March. Available from: https://www.dataversity.net/the-importance-of-data-literacy/# (archived at https://perma.cc/9295-8T9N)

2 Lexico.com, Definition of Read. Lexico.com. Available from: https://www.lexico.com/en/definition/read (archived at https://perma.cc/C4SR-LW6M)

3 Lexico.com, Definition of Work. Lexico.com. Available from: https://www.lexico.com/en/definition/work (archived at https://perma.cc/4RZ3-HWFP)

4 Goodreads.com, Mark Twain Quotes. Goodreads.com. Available from: https://www.goodreads.com/quotes/459791-work-and-play-are-words-used-to-describe-the-same (archived at https://perma.cc/YT5D-ENKM)

5 Lexico.com, Definition of Analysis. Lexico.com. Available from: https://www.lexico.com/en/definition/analysis (archived at https://perma.cc/94SC-D5CH)

6 Lexico.com, Definition of Analysis. Lexico.com. Available from: https://www.lexico.com/en/definition/analysis (archived at https://perma.cc/94SC-D5CH)

7 Lexico.com, Definition of Communicate. Lexico.com. Available from: https://www.lexico.com/en/definition/communicate (archived at https://perma.cc/VC92-CYN3)

04

The data literacy umbrella

Now that we have the definition of data literacy behind us, it is important to understand that data literacy partners with different puzzle pieces that make up different aspects of data and analytical strategy. When done properly, the puzzle can be an amazing picture versus a struggle to reach your vision. For this, data and analytical strategy should be the starting point for organizational work around data and analytics, but, far too often, organizations are not starting here. Once the strategy is in place, then the tools and specifications for data and analytics work can be put in place. Let's explore some of these tools and specifications.

We've covered data literacy, but what about data science? What about data visualization and data governance? Do data ethics play a part within data literacy? In this chapter, we will be covering these different areas of the data and analytical universe, and more. With that in mind, remember that by definition data literacy is the ability to read, work with, analyze, and communicate with data. As we explore different areas within data and analytics, we will approach these areas with both strategy and the four characteristics of data literacy. Specifically, we can look at how each area of data and analytics, and data literacy, work together to achieve holistic success. The areas this chapter will cover are not all-encompassing, but play crucial elements in data and analytics:

FIGURE 4.1   The data literacy umbrella

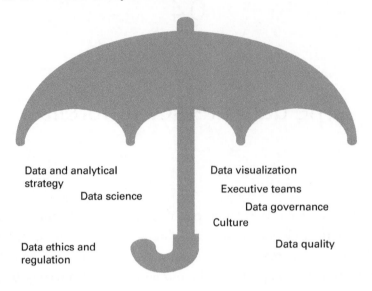

- data and analytical strategy;
- data science;
- data visualization;
- executive teams;
- culture;
- data quality;
- data governance;
- data ethics and regulation.

One thing we will not be covering, as it can be a whole book itself, is a comprehensive data and analytical strategy. In a later chapter we will be covering the topic a bit more than here, but data literacy is absolutely needed for data and analytical success, as without a data literate organization, how can a data and analytical strategy succeed? But, again, that can encompass a book itself; instead, we will cover crucial pieces.

To begin our journey, let us hit the starting line with a brief overview of data and analytical strategy.

Data and analytical strategy

While I am unable to provide a comprehensive outline of data and analytical strategy, I can recommend the great book *Data Strategy* by Bernard Marr. For our purposes, a nice primer will suffice to provide us some more background and sufficient knowledge.

For this primer, I want you to imagine you have been tasked by me to build a house. I come up to you and say, 'Let's build this house', but all I have is a picture of the house and some tools. We don't even know what the interior looks like, but I am super excited for this house. Oh, and by the way, you aren't a construction worker and don't have any experience in building homes, but I have chosen and tasked you with this objective. The good news: I have given you tools, at least. You have some nails, a hammer, the wood, etc., and you set out to work. How successful do you think you would be in achieving the house I want? Oh, did I mention? This is my dream house, so don't disappoint me.

I think we all realize this is an unrealistic approach to achieving success in building a house. Guess what, though? This is what organizations are asking and expecting with data and analytics. Organizations have this idealistic picture in their mind of what they want to achieve with data and analytics. They invest in all these tools and sourcing of data, but what sort of strategy are they using to achieve success? Just like a house is going to find more success with the blueprints, permits, order of operation (i.e. a strategy), so too will data and analytics.

The world of data and analytics is complex, probably much more complex than building me a single house, but the work needs to follow the blueprints or, in other words, a *strategy*. Now we are speaking of data and analytical strategy, we need to understand that the data and analytical strategy is not the end goal. The end goal is the organization's goals and objectives, with data and analytics being tools and enablers to see the organization's success.

When an organization looks to implement a data and analytical strategy, one key element is data literacy. As we were building our home, I mentioned one key thing about you – did you catch it? You are not a construction worker! How many people in your organization, right now, are trained data and analytical workers? When I say trained, I mean *trained*. Most people do not go to school, university, etc., for a background in data and analytics. So, like when I ask you to build a house using just tools and a picture, you are like the many workers in an organization who are trying to make sense of the data placed in front of them, not even able to use analytics as they do not know how. Overall, data and analytical strategies must be in place to include the human element of data literacy.

Data literacy and data science

Data science is, in reality, something that has been around for a very long time. The desire to utilize data to test, understand, experiment, and prove out hypotheses has been around for ages. To put it simply: the use of data to figure things out has been around since a human tried to utilize the information about herds moving about and finding ways to satisfy hunger. The topic of data science came into popular culture more and more as the advent of 'big data' came to the forefront of the business world. How many times have we heard the catchy phrases surrounding big data? Combine the world of big data with the growing production of data, the Internet of Things, and so forth, and data science has become as common a term as others within the dictionary of business. In fact, a fun article from *Harvard Business Review*, published in October 2012, really helped to drive data science into the minds of business: 'Data Scientist: The Sexiest Job of the 21st Century'.[1] Now, how often has someone in the data and statistics field been called sexy? Well, we can rejoice, we were called sexy and our day arrived.

With that quote and the popularity of the 'data scientist', problems started to appear. Suddenly the demand for this highly sought-out role was higher than the actual number of trained data scientists. An article from May 2019 highlighted that 'more than 4,000 data scientist job openings are expected for [2019], according to the report, up 56 per cent from 2018'.[2] What was interesting to me, however, was the article's further poignant point that the shortage of data scientists 'doesn't mean they can't acquire the types of skills data scientists typically possess', which I feel is a very accurate point. However, even if the company did manage to hire a data scientist after convincing themselves they do need one, they then struggled with how to use these data scientists or where to fit them into the big picture, usually from their lack of data and analytical strategy.

With the growing emphasis on STEM (science, technology, engineering, and mathematics) education, more individuals are growing and investing in skills necessary for the data and analytical economy. With the knowledge that the data, digital, and analytical world is upon us already, organizations cannot wait for the workforce to be fully data literate. Especially as, while STEM education is fantastic and should be taught, it does not give a complete picture. The term needs to be expanded to STEAM education, which is: science, technology, engineering, arts, and mathematics. We can never, ever forget the arts within the new data world. The reasons for this necessity can be expansive, but we must remember the power of the human mind. Our abilities as humans to bring creativity, variation, seeing things that maybe a computer can't, can bring power to data and analysis. Plus, the ability we have to bring stories to the data is immense.

Even though more people will develop backgrounds in these fields of STEAM, the aforementioned article from 2019 illustrates a very important point: for years, individuals were not flocking to studies in the fields of data, statistics, quantitative analysis, and so forth. Within this large gap for data science talent, we can fill in the space with the wonderful world of data literacy.

The world of data science plays an extremely important part within the umbrella of data literacy. Data science plays a critical part for the world of data and analytical strategy, and for the four levels of analytics. Data science can build predictions, empowering organizations to use a metaphorical crystal ball to determine direction and decisions. With data science, individuals can utilize the scientific method and other means to test, determine, and find insight while organizations can learn very important pieces to move their needle. Data science is extremely important to the world of data literacy.

First, a personal example. I sat in a meeting with the CEO of a data science company. Remember that this is a data science company. I asked a question similar to this: 'How many data scientists would you have present to your executive team or board?' The CEO put his hand up and with it made a big zero. I don't know if it is really that drastic that we can't ask any data scientists to present or public speak for us. This story does illustrate some of the disparate and separating powers in the data and analytic space. In the past, areas that utilized data and analytics, software and technology, were separate or set in different parts of the organization. Data scientists have been trained in different ways, and communication or public speaking was not stressed and emphasized. So, historically speaking, we haven't asked this of our data scientists. That needs to change, and a strategy needs to include these pieces.

In my travels and work around the world, I am asked: do data scientists have a place within data literacy? I will emphatically say yes! When we think of our data and analytical strategy puzzle, plus the need for organizations to democratize data to the masses, everyone must have the ability to communicate effectively with data. This means the training and education for data scientists will vary away from the beginner who is just getting started with data. We need the data scientist to learn public speaking, ways to communicate effectively, allowing all to partake in the data journey they are embarking on. I am willing to bet, most data scientists have had the chance to share their analyses only to have the audience stare at them like a deer looking into the lights of an oncoming car. When this happens, so many effective insights and thoughts can go unnoticed simply because the audience didn't understand. In this case, data literacy is asking the data scientist to create dialogue, language, and things everyone can understand. Their role needs to evolve in order for them to be able to empower others to be data literate.

How else may data science play into the world of data literacy? Well, if not everyone needs to be a data scientist, but everyone needs to be data literate, where does data science and the technical world play into data literacy? We must, and I stress must, have data science and I mean pure data science, somewhere in the organization. This allows those with these advanced skills to build strong analytical models. Pure data science is the use of data to test, hypothesize, utilize statistics and more, to predict, model, build algorithms, and so forth. This is the technical part of the puzzle. We need this within each organization. By having it, we can utilize the power that these technical aspects bring to data and analytics. Then, with the power to communicate effectively, the analysis can flow throughout the needed parts of an organization.

Data literacy and data visualization

The world of data literacy is vast, with different moving parts, but one area that is available to help simplify and empower everyone is data visualization. What is data visualization? Data visualization is a simplified approach to studying data. Imagine you are given the task to analyze a table of 100,000 rows of data, and 50 columns. How many of us would jump at that opportunity? Data visualization is taking the massive amounts of data and simplifying it into a visualization, where our visual skill can come into play to help us with our data and information. To help us get moving on data visualization, a few examples can help set the tone for us.

Figure 4.2 shows one of my favorite data visualizations of all time. We can follow Napoleon's march into Russia and see how the army dwindled over time, simplifying the information. Can you imagine if the data and information was presented to you in a tabular format or from original journals? What if all this data was found in different journals and you had to piece it together? How much fun would you have trying to decipher what happened to the army? This data visualization helps to simplify the march and information for us.

FIGURE 4.2 Visualization: Charles Joseph Minard's 1869 map of Napoleon's march on Russia

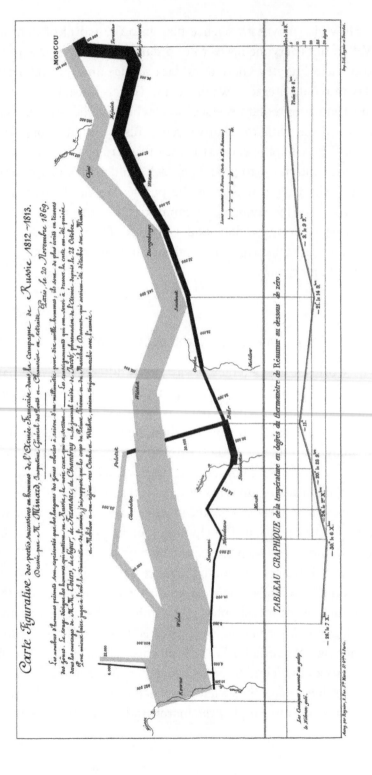

FIGURE 4.3   Visualization: John Snow's 1854 Broad Street cholera outbreak map

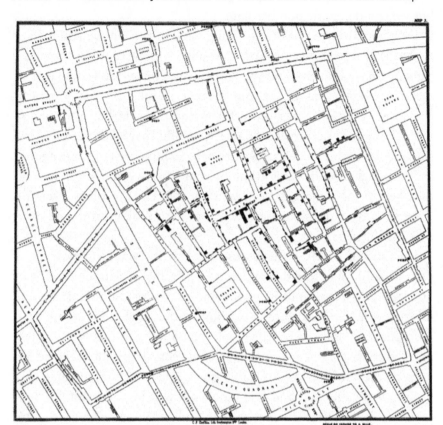

Have you ever reviewed the map of the post-cholera outbreak that occurred in England in the 1800s, shown in Figure 4.3? This is a very interesting case study where data visualization helped a community to halt a cholera outbreak that could have been much worse and lasted longer. Through the power of visualizing the data, the community was able to determine that gathering water from the same spot, by multiple people, was the issue and caused the outbreak. With this new information, the community was able to find causation and implement changes to stop the outbreak. Isn't the power of visualizing data and information amazing?

With these visualizations in mind, we can see what simplifying data and information can do for the story, but just what is data visualization? We don't need to dig too much further into data visualizations themselves, as you can pick up the book *The Big Book of Dashboards* by Steve Wexler, Jeffrey Shaffer, and Andy Cotgrave, but we can define them more here.

Data visualization has roots going back in time, if we really want to get to the details of this art. Our ancestors were using visualizations to share information and stories. We can see stories shared in the hieroglyphics of Egypt and ancient peoples on the American continent. How did this powerful method of sharing information find its way into the world of data? We could share stories of the first statistical measurement that was visualized hundreds of years ago, or share thoughts on the first graph or chart, but we aren't going to do that here; that topic has been written about many times over. We want to jump into the modern world of data visualization and business intelligence.

Let's start this part of the discussion off with a question: how many of you would like to sift through a large table of data consisting of 100,000 plus rows and 50 plus columns, to find some insight and information? I would stare at my boss with a crazy look in my eyes. I am guessing not many of us would be jumping at this opportunity, and rightfully so. Even if you found some sort of insight at the beginning of the table, what if 24,000 rows and 13 columns later that insight was debunked and you didn't know it because you don't go past row 174? Just following the rows and columns mentioned here can be confusing. Yes, this is a very hypothetical example and one where I don't think any of us will find ourselves in the near future.

Now, what if I told you there is a powerful way we could simplify that table to help you and your organization to describe what has happened (descriptive analytics) and work towards insight (diagnostic analytics)? This is the power of data visualization. Data visualization simplifies the massive amounts of data that organizations are collecting and producing, but not only that, data visualization plays a very important part in data literacy and its impact with the four levels of analytics. How does it do this? I can hear you asking me that question right now. Let me show you.

First, let's look at data visualization with its impact to data literacy and the story we will share will be all too familiar. Remember, the definition of data literacy is the ability to read, work with, analyze, and communicate with data. When we ask how many of us are going to university and college for studies in statistics, mathematics, and so forth, the answer is not many. When organizations then look to democratize data, most are not going to be able to absorb the data and information, so we need software to help us simplify. In steps the powerful data and analytics tool: data visualization. Companies such as Qlik, Tableau, and ThoughtSpot (to name a few) all share and empower individuals to visualize and simplify data. Here, individuals can read the data in a simpler manner, it can be easier to work with it, asking the right questions can help and finally communicating with impactful data visualizations can move the needle for us. This allows the mass of users to visually see the data, find insight, and work through the four levels of analytics. 'How?' you may say. I am so glad you asked.

When we delve into the four levels of analytics, the first level is particularly impacted by data visualizations. Remember, the first level of analytics is descriptive analytics, where we are describing what happened in the past or what is currently happening. How can we describe what happened if we are gathering millions upon millions of data points? Here is a perfect example for the power of visualizing an organizations data. When we take the millions of data points, we can gather them into trending charts, compelling visualizations that help us ask questions to 'why' things are happening.

The second level of analytics is diagnostic analytics and is greatly helped by the world of data visualization. Remember, diagnostic analytics is the insight level of analytics, where we figure out 'why' something happened. Data visualization can be the catalyst that sparks questions: Why is this outlier here? Why is this data point so far from the others? I see this bar in the bar chart is so much taller than the others; what category is that, and why is it taller? I see this cluster of data points all fall within this time frame, but why are there some that are outside the desired time period? All of these hypothetical questions come about because we can see the data visualized in front of us, allowing us to ask the questions (the third characteristic in the definition of data literacy) that will help us find the insight to allow us to move our organization's needle. Then, we can start to make more and more predictions.

In steps the third level of analytics: predictive analytics. With a data visualization in front of us, maybe particularly with a line chart, we can see where things are trending and heading. With data literacy, we are able to read the information in front of us, work with the data to manipulate and get different views of the data visualization by slicing and dicing the data, and then analyze the information with questions. With all of these points, finding some insight and then pulling potential levers for the business, we can utilize the data visualization to predict where the company and organization are going to head. We will use an example line chart to illustrate this point (Figure 4.4).

In our visualization, we can see different lines represented by different states: Arizona, Idaho, and Utah. Each of these lines has trends that are moving in an upward direction. We have the 'descriptive analytic' showing us what the population has been over the last few decades. Second, this can spur questions for us: Why is Arizona growing fast? What factors are driving these growth rates? Maybe it is Arizona's warm weather year round or a boom in jobs. Whatever the reasons, we have insight that can lead us to predictive analytics.

FIGURE 4.4   Example line chart

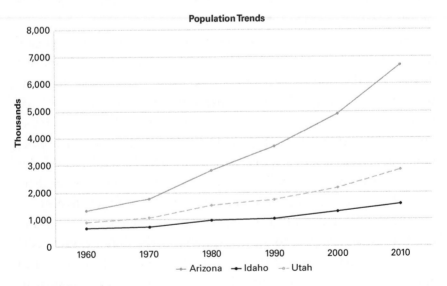

SOURCE US Census data

In our case, the predictive model can show us where the population will be by 2020, the year of the next census data and time period.

With prescriptive analytics, where the data and technology are driving the analytics and insight themselves, the power of data visualization can be utilized to show us what those predictions are. Then, we can start processes over and over again within the four levels of analytics.

Overall, data visualization has a very significant place within the world of data literacy. Data literacy is for the masses, and data visualization is powerful to simplify what could be very complicated. Each of us has the power to really harness the power of data visualization in our lives to further our careers and help our organizations thrive in the data and analytical world.

Data literacy and executive teams

One may ask: what kind of role do executive teams play within data literacy? Besides being those who should own the data and analytical strategy, plus driving the investment, executives have a key part to play within data literacy. The answer to that is very simple and it comes in two different pieces: executives must be data literate themselves and executives must help drive the data literacy initiative within their own organization.

Executives themselves must be data literate, even in their busy schedules. Executives must utilize the power of reading different dashboards and reports possessing many data points. Think of the world of key performance indicators, or KPIs. Are these not points of data and analytics? Yes! So they need to be data literate.

Along with reading data, executives should possess the ability to work with data. Now, think about that last point for a minute: how much time does an executive have to really work with data? Enough! Working with data can mean as simple as receiving the weekly KPI dashboard and quickly reviewing it. We need to change our mindsets of thinking working with data needs to be complex and require technical skills. By simple receiving and reading the weekly KPI dashboard, an executive is working with data.

Moving beyond working with data, executives absolutely need to be able to analyze data to further their organization's goals and visions. When an executive reads and works with data, the ability to analyze and ask strong questions of the data and information presented to them is imperative. As executives work through the data and look for answers, the ability to ask questions of what is presented to them can help spark analysis and more. This skill is crucial for an executive, especially with their limited time and busy schedules.

Finally, executives absolutely must be able to communicate with data in a clear, concise, and powerful manner. By possessing the ability to communicate in an effective manner, executives can express their thoughts and ideas with regards to the data and analysis presented to them. Do we really want an executive who is bumbling over words and can't share the data and vision they have constructed? I hope not!

With understanding how executives utilize the four characteristics of data literacy we can venture into one key and pivotal reason why executives need to be data literate: executives set the tone for an organization, including the goals and vision of the organization. Along with the overall goals of the organization, the executive team will sign off the data and analytical strategy to be deployed. Do we want a data and analytical vision driven by those not skilled in data and analytics? I hope not! We need a strong, data literate executive team to ensure the strategy is powerful, impactful, and ties back to the organizational goals.

Along with the important information that executives need to be data literate, there is one other key role they play: executives drive data literacy learning and initiatives at the organization. As we have seen, there is a large skills gap within the world of data and analytics. For organizations to capitalize on data, they must run data literacy learning, empowerment, and initiatives. Executives need to invest in and empower their workforces to develop the skills needed to help data and analytical strategy succeed. When executives do this, the workforce will be more self-sufficient and empowered to truly move the needle.

Overall, executives need to invest in and empower themselves with data literacy skills to ensure they are making smart, data informed decisions, and to ensure the workforce has a strong data literacy initiative where the entire workforce is empowered to succeed. Again, we are seeing how everyone has a strong part within data literacy.

Data literacy and culture

If there is one key obstacle to success with data and analytical strategies, the one at the top of the list is culture. Wait, would not sourcing data be a bigger obstacle, or how about software and technology adoption? The reality is yes, those are big obstacles, but culture is the number one thing standing in the way of an organization succeeding with data and analytical strategies. With that in mind, ok then, we can just change the culture and be set and ready to roll, correct?

How many of us have ever said to ourselves: changing an organization's culture is easy? Well, that same person probably would say climbing Mount Everest without training, acclimatizing to the region, or oxygen tanks is a piece of cake, or that running an ultra-marathon without training in any way is also a simple task. The reality is, changing an organization's culture is not an easy task. So, how does an organization adopt and utilize data and analytical strategies if the culture isn't ready? That is a million-dollar question, one that can require many steps and processes to implement. One key piece to that puzzle can be data literacy.

When one thinks of the wide range of skills and abilities we have used to describe data literacy, it should be clear there is not just one set of skills that each individual needs to obtain to ensure pure data literacy. One individual can obtain strong skills in asking questions, while another develops strong skills in telling stories, and yet another masters the art of data visualization. By each individual harnessing a combination of their personal talents and abilities, with development in data literacy, holistically the organization can thrive with data. By helping individuals develop skills in data literacy and the ability to harness the power of data, the organization is developing the ability to succeed with data and analytical strategies. You may be asking: how does this help the culture? I am so glad you asked.

How many of us have heard the phrase 'I have always done it this way and I don't want to change', or some variation of the same? This is a common phrase in the world of business and our lives in general. We get comfortable doing the same thing repeatedly. As such, individuals and organizational cultures around the world don't necessarily want to 'change', and perceive it as a thing to fear. The wonderful thing about data literacy is it is not asking for a change in how things are done, but an enhancement. Another question or thought we may hear often from individuals in their careers: 'Is there an easier way to do this'? or 'I wish this could be done differently'. In steps data literacy.

Data literacy is not a change in an individual's abilities, talents, or skills within their careers, but more of an enhancement and empowerment of the individual to succeed with data. When it comes to data and analytics succeeding in an organization's culture, the increase in the workforces' skills with data literacy will help individuals to succeed with the strategy laid in front of them. In this way, organizations are not trying to run large change management programs; the process is more of an evolution and strengthening of individual's talents with data. When we help individuals do more with data, we in turn help the organization's culture do more with data.

Data literacy and data quality

Data quality is a very important part of data and analytical work, plus data literacy. To understand this part of the puzzle, we can look to using a recipe. How many of us have a favorite meal that we just love? For me, personally, I love good sushi. With sushi, there are certain combinations and things that go into the different rolls that make the flavor stand out and pop. What if the combinations were followed correctly, but the ingredients were not fresh, were old, and of poor quality? When you take that first bite, do you think your taste buds will be jumping for joy? I am guessing you know the answer to that. The same can be said with data and analytical work.

When we are working hard to utilize data to make smarter decisions, we need quality ingredients to make it happen. This is also a key to data literacy and data quality working together: if an individual is not confident in their data literacy skills, could they know the data seems 'off' or is not of quality? Also, what if they are not confident with their data literacy skills and they poorly communicate with the data team itself, causing poor data to be used? I think data quality and data literacy are such a simplistic concept that we don't need to dig in further – just remember that data quality is an imperative to data and analytical success.

Data literacy and data governance

First off, what in the world is data governance? To help us start on a level playing field, ensuring we understand how we are defining data governance is key. Dataversity provides a clear definition of data governance:

> Data Governance is a collection of practices and processes which help to ensure the formal management of data assets within an organization. Data Governance often includes other concepts such as Data Stewardship, Data Quality, and others to help an enterprise gain better control over its data assets, including methods, technologies, and behaviors around the proper management of data. It also deals with security and privacy, integrity, usability, integration, compliance, availability, roles and responsibilities, and overall management of the internal and external data flows within an organization.[3]

Simply put, data governance is the governing of the organization's data. That seems straightforward, but what does data literacy have to do with data governance?

First, those who are running the data governance strategies, putting the rules and practices in place, and ensuring the organization's data is protected most assuredly have to be data literate. This goes back to an earlier point with executives and how they are in charge of an organization's data vision and strategy and must be data literate to ensure a strong strategy. The same is true of the data governance team. If the data governance team is not data literate, well, I think we could run into many, many issues with the data and how it is being used within an organization.

Second, as those who are using the data are trying to gain access and utilize data in their job functions and roles, if they are not data literate, they may not understand why they are able to get access to some data and not others. This can cause a plethora of problems, such as infighting within the organization and data isolation, as groups don't want to share the data they are using. Overall, the workforce must be data literate to ensure the proper data governance strategies are implemented correctly and succeed.

Third, looking at the definition provided by Dataversity, data governance can encompass other key principles: data stewardship, data quality, and so forth. Data literacy empowers individuals in all of these cases: being good stewards, ensuring people know what quality is and why it matters, and so forth. Data literacy truly empowers individuals to understand these key principles.

Fourth, and finally, data literacy helps individuals to understand the technology and software invested in to help drive data and analytic strategies. When individuals understand data through data literacy, then the strategies and technology to help them succeed are put in front them, they understand how it works, and why it is being used this way.

Overall, data governance is a vital way for organizations to succeed with data and analytics, and data literacy helps to empower individuals to succeed with governance.

Data literacy and ethics and regulation

As the world has needed to adapt to the increase in data production, data usage, and, in fact, social media's advancement in data, more and more laws and thoughts are popping up within the world of regulating data. We have seen laws passed such as the General Data

Protection Regulation (GDPR) from the European Union, which looks to regulate and protect data. We have seen concerns thrown out regarding the ethical use of aptly named 'black box' algorithms, where there have been found biased, prejudice, and even racist results. Throughout all of this, stronger conversations have popped up asking what is to be done with all of this? In can step the amazing world of data literacy. To help us see just how data literacy can impact the world of ethics, let's look at real-world examples of data usage and how data literacy can empower us to know what is happening.

Example 1: Our personal data usage

How many of us have had the opportunity to sign up for a new website and we have to create a new login? I hope we are all raising our hands right now. Within this process, a lot of times we see the 'create a new login' option or other options that allow us to log in using different channels, such as a Google or Facebook channel. When we create a new login utilizing one of these other channels, the sharing of data between the new site and our existing sites can occur. Now, some people may know this, but a lot do not or didn't know when they signed up. Data literacy is a direct benefit here.

When we are empowered with skills in data literacy, we have the ability to understand where our data is going, how it is being utilized, and so forth. Then, we can make smarter, data literacy informed decisions with regards to how we log in, create accounts and so forth. Data literacy gives a direct empowerment towards our personal data usage.

Example 2: Algorithm usage

Have you heard of the term 'black box' algorithm? This is a term that has become prevalent in the world. It means an algorithm that is built and lacks transparency from others to see into its processes, codes, and so forth. Essentially, a black box algorithm is a mysterious way in which an algorithm is used to derive data that is utilized in many industries. Some of these industries can include hiring practices at organizations, banking, and finance in determining a person's worthiness for a loan, and so forth. How does data literacy help in this case?

Data literacy empowers us to know the usage of data and how an algorithm can potentially be misleading, biased, and so forth; data literacy empowers us with the right type of skepticism that is needed to question everything. For example: imagine an algorithm gives us a result, telling us we are not able to get a loan because of the zip code we live in. What if we have great credit, a strong job, and so forth, and the one issue is the zip code? The algorithm is only looking at this one factor, but because of it, we aren't set for the loan. With data literacy we can ask: Does this seem right? Can machine learning really take external factors into place and make smart decisions? Should we get rid of algorithms altogether?

The answer to the last question is *no*! Algorithms have power, but we can't just believe everything they say. We need the power of the human element, data literacy, to help us decipher the results and ensure the information gathered and shared leads to the right course of action.

Example 3: Implementation of regulations

When new regulations are presented to us, like GDPR from the European Union, it can be difficult for the masses to implement them because, to be frank, they have no clue what it is saying. Data literacy empowers us as individuals to understand the rules and regulations as they are presented to us. Data literacy also empowers us to help implement these regulations as they go into effect. Let's look at GDPR as a prime example of how data literacy can put this regulation into place.

When GDPR first rolled out, individuals working in industries that were more affected, potentially in banking as they needed to implement new rules and disclosures, could have found it hard to put new policies in place, as they were unfamiliar with 'why' they needed to. Instead, they just did as told, without understanding the purpose. In steps data literacy.

When individuals are data literate, GDPR doesn't present as big a challenge as it would with a lack of data literacy. With a data literate workforce or individual, the implementation can run in a smoother fashion, plus the individuals tasked with putting the rules and logic into place can help others understand the 'why' behind it. I remember this law going into place and seeing more and more disclosures popping up and needing my acceptance. I knew what was happening, so I was more than happy to sign the disclosure and move on. For others who don't necessarily work in the data field, they may have experienced a disruption to their normal routine, questioning more and more why they have to sign this waver or that one. This disruption can cause a disruption of service from organizations, as more people have questions. With a stronger workforce set up with data literacy skills, the rollout can take effect from a much more intelligent perspective. Both organizations and society benefit from data literacy, as the rollout of regulations on data can happen from a smoother perspective.

Example 4: Ethical use of data

What about our personal use of data to make decisions? What kind of ethics do we need to abide by to ensure our use is structured correctly and successful? We can see over and over again where a person's bias is built into their decision-making processes with regards to data. I mean, look at politics as a whole and we don't need any further examples. How does data literacy help us to ensure we are able to account for and work to eliminate bias in our decisions with data? How does data literacy ensure we are ethically using data in general?

The world of data is fraught with scams, unethical decision-making, and skewing data to fit our own narrative. Data literacy and our own ability to understand where we are misusing data for our own purposes allows us to work towards stronger decisions. With data literacy, we should be able to see where we are and could be going wrong. With data literacy, we should be able to question everything from a strong position, allowing us to understand if we are biased in our decisions or using data unethically. With data literacy, we can also decipher where others are possibly using data to make a point but aren't showing us the whole picture. I mean, politics and the media may be two of the most nefarious users of this last one.

Data literacy truly allows us to see where data is being used ethically or unethically, and we need to empower ourselves with this skill so we can help move the needle forward for society.

Overall, when it comes to ethics and regulations regarding data, the world is only in its infant stages. We are seeing more and more attempts and successes with regards to regulating data. In order for these types of programs to succeed, we can't just put rules and laws into place, we have to ensure individuals are empowered and strong in their data literacy skills. Doing so helps individuals to see the importance of these rules and ensure they are utilizing data effectively.

Chapter summary

As we saw in the first chapter, the world of data is quite expansive and is not slowing down. The world of data literacy is also quite large, with many different facets and topics that are encompassed therein. Overall, data and analytical strategy should start an organization's data and analytical journey. From there, different facets come into play to build the brilliant picture contained in the puzzle.

In our discussion in this chapter, we covered the topic of data literacy from the standpoint of the data literacy umbrella. This umbrella is not meant to be comprehensive, but a strong showing of different areas within data literacy. Although it is not a comprehensive list of all topics within data literacy, it does show the breadth and depth of this immensely powerful topic. As we learn and explore more of this topic, we can bring it back to these different areas and more, helping us to think of the many different areas it can encompass.

Notes

1 Davenport, T and Patil, D J (2012) Data Scientist: The Sexiest Job of the 21st Century, *Harvard Business Review*, October issue. Available from: https://hbr.org/2012/10/data-scientist-the-sexiest-job-of-the-21st-century (archived at https://perma.cc/44AP-9T2M)

2 Violino, B (2019) 6 Ways to Deal with the Great Data Scientist Shortage, CIO, 22 May. Available from: https://www.cio.com/article/3397137/6-ways-to-deal-with-the-great-data-scientist-shortage.html (archived at https://perma.cc/JDD8-6CQU)

3 Knight, M (2017) What is Data Governance? Dataversity.net, 18 December. Available from: https://www.dataversity.net/what-is-data-governance/ (archived at https://perma.cc/YZ9D-P2KC)

05

Reading and speaking the language of data

When we think of the definition of data literacy, which gives to us four characteristics to be aware of – the ability to read, work with, analyze, and communicate with data – one of these characteristics may stand out above the others. I am often asked: 'Which of the four characteristics is the most important?' In reality, as we can imagine, they are all important, but that is a disingenuous answer when I feel one rises above the others: the ability to read data. The ability to read anything, in general, is a freeing ability, allowing us to decipher, learn, and come up with ideas on our own. Reading also allows us to understand what is happening. With data, this ability to read is vital, as it means an individual can look at the data and information, and then can comprehend what is in front of them. With the ability to read, individuals can also then translate this into the ability to speak the language of data. The ability to speak the language of data helps individuals comprehend and figure out what is in front of them, and to communicate their discoveries. I feel a story or illustration can help us to illuminate what we are discussing.

Imagine you have planned an amazing vacation that is coming up in the near future. This is a vacation you have been excited about for a long time as it is on your bucket list and is a top destination for you. As part of your heightening anticipation, you have put forth the effort to dig in and study the activities to engage in, and the locations and restaurants to visit (the food is the best part, right?). In essence, you have invested money and time to prepare for a nice vacation.

As part of your preparation, you decide to not wing it and instead you build a strategy surrounding key goals for the vacation: departure and return dates, hotels to stay in, transportation costs and accessibility (such as public transit versus a rental car), currency exchange, and so forth. This preparation helps you to think you are all set; and you are beyond excited for this once-in-a-lifetime vacation and eager for the trip to occur.

As the time approaches, you prepare to arrive at the airport and check in early enough to get a good meal before your long, long flight. You settle into your seat with a smile on your face, a snack in your hand, and earphones in to help you drift off for a nap. The plane takes off, and you close your eyes with dreams of vacation joy on your mind. When the plane touches down in the destination city, you are eager and excited to jump off, make it through passport control, and grab your bags, ready to find the nearest taxi to take you into the city. As we all know, this last part always goes perfectly smoothly... so we are going to imagine it goes spectacularly well and you open the door to your taxi.

As you get in the taxi, the taxi driver starts to speak to you in their native language, the native language of the country. You start to stress a little because the driver does not speak your native tongue at all, and you aren't understanding the driver very well. Eventually, you communicate well enough to get your message across: where your hotel is located, and that you want to go there. Throughout the taxi ride to the hotel, you tell yourself over and over that the language won't be a barrier, everything will be great.

As you arrive at the hotel, a person opens your door, helps you to the front desk, and you start the check-in process. Once again, this person doesn't speak your native tongue very well, but at least this time they understand and speak enough to help you out. You get into your room, eager to venture into the city. As you leave for the city, you start to notice that there isn't much written in your native tongue (thank goodness for Google Maps and GPS, right?). You walk around, excited to try some local cuisine and enter a few restaurants, hoping to enjoy it, only to find out they don't speak your tongue, the menu is only in the local language, and you start to get frustrated. The same thing happens in different areas on this vacation. What you had planned as an amazing vacation ends in what can only be summed up as a disaster. How could this have happened and what in the world does it have to do with data literacy? Everything!

When organizations implement their data and analytical strategies, the ability of the workforce to understand that strategy is crucial. A lack of ability by an organization to read and understand data can be a strong frustration point to adoption and success. While this lack of reading and understanding isn't the only problem, it can cause mass confusion and frustration. How many organizations and individuals trying to succeed with data and analytics are running into these understanding problems? First and foremost, a lot of organizations and individuals do not have as solid a plan to utilize data and analytics as you did on your vacation. Second, a lot of companies struggle when trying to succeed with data and analytics because those across the organization do not speak a common language with data and analytics; what we will call 'data fluency'. I mean, think about it: could there be another language in business with a more convoluted vocabulary than data and analytics? Let's look at some of the words or acronyms that make up this complex language: ODAP, OLAP, Markov Chain Analysis, data schemes, star schemas, big data, business intelligence, artificial intelligence, augmented intelligence, structured and unstructured data, statistics, Bayesian statistics, probability, and so forth. This is just a portion of that list! Is it any wonder people aren't flocking to memorize all these words?

Now, imagine your organization is setting forth this powerful strategy, going into the world of data and analytics with full steam and intentions to build a strong plan and vision, in other words, the plane has landed. Your organization is excited at the possibilities that data and analytics bring to the table. The organization invests in solid data sourcing, technology to be used, data quality, and so forth. The organization sets out on its data adventure, only to find people are walking around confused, struggling to hold meaningful conversations, and a lot of conversations have at least one in the party staring back at the speaker with wide eyes as they daydream about their next meal.

Data literacy and data fluency play a critical role in the success of data and analytical strategy. In fact, we may just call data fluency or this ability to speak the language of data the secret ingredient within the world of data and analytics. Imagine if we can get everyone in the organization comfortable with speaking the same language of data and analytics? The free flow of data and information, of analysis, and more, is a powerful way to help data and analytics succeed. Imagine how powerful that would be to a workforce. Now, notice I didn't say everyone needs to speak it fluently in the exact same way. No, no, no, that should not be the plan. Imagine if your organization told you to learn the whole vocabulary that the statisticians in your organization use. Imagine if they said you needed to learn the full language of coding that your developers know. How many of you would jump at the opportunity and say: 'Let's do this'? (Now some of you may be statisticians and more than happy to have everyone learn your vocabulary, but alas, I am sorry, that is not what we are doing here.)

It should not be the plan to teach everyone the exact same language and abilities. Instead, we should imagine if we help everyone in the organization to be comfortable speaking the same language. This does not mean we all are at the same level. Just like in a civilization speaking a language. We want to enable everyone to have confidence to communicate with others. This means that some people will be advanced in the language, some will have a smaller vocabulary, but that data fluency can flow throughout the organization; this is about enabling the organization to have conversations around data and seeing fewer 'deer in the headlights' expressions on people's faces. Not only does this ability to speak the language help data and analytics to flow better, it helps enhance the first characteristic of data literacy: reading data. Overall, individuals and organizations will see data and analytics improve.

To help us understand data literacy and the amazing power reading data and data fluency have on data analytical success, we will dive into these topics:

- reading data;
- defining data fluency and what it can mean for the organization;

- a data dictionary;

- strategies organizations can adopt to improve data fluency.

Finally, we will walk through an example analysis and decision driven by data, allowing us to see the flow of conversation and reading data throughout a data and analytical process.

Reading data

We explored the world of reading data in Chapter 3, so we don't want to repeat the point again here. What will help us to expand upon the definition of reading data are real-world examples of the ability to read data and its impact on either an organization, individual, or society. To do this, let's jump into some different examples of where reading data has empowered some sort of success or outcome. The three examples we will cover include the use of data to drive risk management, the power of data at the US Open Tennis Championship, and the tasty power of data with Coca-Cola.

Our first example takes us into the world of risk management, which, in the digital world that we live in, is a vital skill and process for organizations. How often are we hearing about ethics within data and analytics? How often do we hear about privacy within data? We hear these things quite often. Possessing skills within data and analytics in risk management is necessary in the mitigation of risky moves, ventures, and so forth. Being able to communicate this throughout an organization, especially one like a financial institution, is vital. The example we want to dive into is the United Overseas Bank (UOB) bank from Singapore... who knew a bank uses data to help in risk management (I hope they use data to drive risk management)?[1]

In our example, the UOB uses data to help one of its processes go from 18 hours down to a few minutes. Isn't the power of data amazing? Through this ability, the bank has the ability to drive more real-time analytics. This offers up a question I get asked quite regularly: will data and analytics, the empowerment it can bring, make us lazy? I like to say this: if a process took 18 hours and now only takes a few minutes, think about the freeing up of your time this brings for proper analysis. This is one of the vital reasons data literacy needs to be present in an organization.

Now this speeding up of time can raise another interesting question: what could the organization do if the people couldn't read the data and information being presented? Herein we can see the power of reading data. Again, reading data is the ability to look at the information and comprehend what is being said. With this ability to read data, the strategies the bank has put in place to utilize data for analytical success have a higher chance to reach their potential. Then, as things are implemented, reading data allows the workforce to help implement the proper changes and move the needle. This all can come about with a strong data literacy initiative at the organization.

Next, let's jump in and look at a fun use of data to enhance the experience for sports fans: the US Open tennis tournament. The US Open, one of the largest tournaments in tennis, is held annually. The US Open pits some of the best tennis players against each other and the event is looking for ways to enhance, improve, and make better the 'fan experience'. Being a sports fan myself, I know that having a strong and fun 'fan experience' really can make memories and help individuals attach to an event. Ask yourself: have you ever been to a big sporting event? I would guess most of us have, and love the atmosphere, excitement, and being there for our teams. What if these experiences could be enhanced and more exciting from the use of data and analytics? That is what the US Open and IBM are doing by teaming up and making the experience better for the fans.[2]

With its work, IBM Watson is driving knowledge, information, and experience to the fans that they might not have seen before. Using artificial intelligence, the fan will now be able to know more about the game of tennis, places to go and visit during the event, and, finally, will curate highlights for the fans. Along with helping the fans, analytics can help drive success for the players. Now, maybe some of us will say this is taking the purity out of the game, but now data and analytics can tell players how much exertion they have put into the match during their play. Isn't that powerful? They can use data to understand more and more about how they are playing. Tennis is definitely not the only sport looking to put data and analytics to use to better its athletes.

Overall, we can see the power of the ability to read data come through in the US Open tennis tournament, from the coaches and players understanding where they are in their efforts, to fans being able to understand the information put in front of them to enhance their experiment. Only one more example is left to study reading data: your favorite soda company and mine (and please, Pepsi fans, don't get too upset), Coca-Cola.

One can ask: how can reading data enhance and help Coca-Cola? As we jump in to see and understand these processes, let's also see where other organizations can apply similar techniques in their businesses. To start, we will look at some specific examples of how Coca-Cola is dealing with data and utilizing it for powering its organization.[3] Example 1: when Coca-Cola launched Cherry Sprite it was a direct result of data collection. Customers would order a soft drink and use the flavor shots to enhance their choice. Through gaining insight and information, a new flavor could be born. Example 2: Coca-Cola is using artificial intelligence bots, essential smart little machines, to help with discussions with customers. In this case, the artificial intelligence bot was part of a vending machine, helping the customer mix their drink exactly how they wanted it. What a great way to understand and learn different mix flavors to enhance the customer experience. Example 3: Coca-Cola uses social media to understand how the products are shown through different social media channels. By using unstructured data like social media, the company can understand how its larger audiences are thinking about, sharing, and using its products. These examples are just three ways into how the great organization of Coca-Cola is using data to stay on top and be recognized as one of the world's top brands.[4]

We have now explored three examples of using data in an organization or event: for risk management, to drive a better fan experience at the US Open tennis tournament, and finally at Coca-Cola. By examining these different real-world examples, we can see how organizations benefit from directly reading data. There are other examples of reading data that you can find in organizations:

- following trends and patterns on marketing campaigns, and understanding how the organization's marketing is succeeding in different conditions;
- understanding the demographics that make up an organization's customer base;
- understanding the different market trends that allow an organization to make new products and release those products at the correct timing, and helping the organization understand how the new release is succeeding or failing in the market.

Overall, reading data is such a powerful way for organizations to embrace and succeed with data literacy initiatives. By empowering the workforce with confidence in looking at data and information, and understanding it, we can create a quick elevation in an organization's data and analytical success.

Data fluency

To begin our study of the world of data fluency, let's go back to when we were babies and learning to talk and read. In reality, we do not need to back that far, but principles and concepts from early language and speaking development can help; we do want to embrace the thoughts that go along with speaking a language, tying us back to the beginning of this chapter. Do you remember that stellar vacation we were planning? How did that go for us again? Unfortunately, it did not go as well as we had hoped. Our vacation was hampered by our lack of ability to speak the native language. That is what is happening in organizations all over. Organizations have grand ideas of data and analytics, what can be achieved, and so forth, but they are running into walls and roadblocks because of lack of understanding. Thankfully, there is a great tool and tactic to help organizations overcome these obstacles and it comes in the simplest form of data fluency.

Data fluency, as defined in this book, is the ability to speak and understand the language of data; it is essentially an ability to communicate with and about data. In different cases around the world, the term data fluency has sometimes been used interchangeably with data literacy. That is not the approach of this book. This book looks to define data literacy as the ability to read, work with, analyze, and communicate with data. Data fluency is the ability to speak and understand the language of data. As you may have guessed it, data fluency plays a direct part in the last part of the definition of data literacy: communicating with data. To help us understand the power of data fluency, though, we are going to tie the ability to speak the language of data to all four characteristics of the definition of data literacy. From this standpoint, we will see how data fluency is a powerful way for an organization to work through data literacy and how data fluency is a key ingredient in this overall strategy.

First, a jump in to see what speaking and understanding the language of data means; let's find out what data fluency means. To help our understanding, we can think back to a time when we were trying to explain something to someone, only to have the person looking back at us look with a confused expression. Have you ever been in a conversation like that? Forget a conversation about data and analytics, just think about a conversation in general: have you ever been talking to someone and within 30–45 seconds that person has glazed over, and you know you have lost them? Why is it that we lose people in conversations? What can we do to ensure our message is getting through?

This is key in the world of data fluency. Organizations develop and enable a common practice and use of language surrounding data. As an organization starts to develop this common language of data, then the conversations about data can drive more decisions. The reason for this is because more people understand what is being said. Historically, and maybe still, these conversations made it difficult to generate results or action. In a lot of cases, this could be because the audience did not understand what was being said. Now, with data fluency, this common language of data being spoken, the conversations can be seen as empowering. The whole of the organization is able to communicate effectively with data, driving the insight and power to move forward with data informed decisions.

We can look to a small example to see how this works. Imagine if a data scientist has conducted an analysis that produced a strong result. With data fluency, the masses of the workforce understand what was done and can implement insight and decisions from the analysis. Another example: imagine if a data analyst has conducted a strong project and is now presenting to the executive team, hoping to get executive buy-in on a new project. With a common data language, the executive can have an easier time understanding the new project (I am sure we all hope to have our projects or requests understood by leadership). Finally, imagine there is a free flow of information throughout the organization because of a common language in data and analytics, so projects, analyses, and strategies can be implemented by all. This is a crucial element for organizations to see data and analytical strategy success.

Overall, this ability of the organization to freely communicate data and information is not just a nice to have, it is an imperative. Figure 5.1 should help open our minds more to the power of data fluency. As can be seen, there is a free flow of information. From the data scientist to the data analysts to the decision-makers to the executive team

FIGURE 5.1 Data fluency in an organization

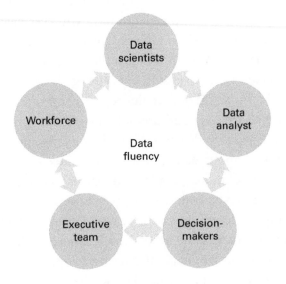

and finally to the workforce, we can see that the free flow of information is amazing for the organizational success within data and analytical strategy. We shouldn't have one thing stand in the way of our data and analytic success: data fluency. Utilize the ability to speak the same language to help drive data and analytical success.

The data dictionary

To help an organization establish a common language in data, a data dictionary can be a strong help. 'Data dictionaries are used to provide detailed information about the contents of a dataset or database, such as the names of measured variables, their data types or formats, and text descriptions. A data dictionary provides a concise guide to understanding and using the data.'[5] This definition, or purpose, describes well what a data dictionary is and what it should be used for. Let me use an example from my career where an individual did not use the data dictionary, nor follow strong practices with data fluency.

In this example, I was in charge of running a large business intelligence group for a financial services provider. My team and I were tasked with building dashboards for our end users, building a data dictionary, and being the source system of record. That is the key: we were supposed to be the source system of record. In our data, we had many metrics and were using them to build strong dashboards for the team.

One day I received an email or call from the executive assistant to the president of the US consumer group. In the conversation, she asked me about a metric or two, trying to figure out what our metrics were showing versus what was provided by the employee. In other words, an employee shared a metric that we provide, but the number they provided did not tie to our number; they got the number somewhere else. In this case, the individual could ask others they knew to get a quick result or response, or if they were skilled in coding at all, they could pull the number themselves. That doesn't seem too bad, does it? The problem was they didn't use our definition of the metric at hand and provided the metric incorrectly. This issue was exacerbated even more, as this number went to the 'street', or was made public, in other words. So, now the team was trying to scramble and figure it out how to mitigate the problem that had occurred.

How was this a poor practice of data fluency? First, the individual did not consult the data dictionary we had built to find out how we were defining certain metrics. By doing this, they put up a roadblock to getting the right answer, because they did not get the information pulled according to the correct definition. Second, they didn't communicate well the impact of the numbers or understand the down road impact these numbers could have by communicating the source and data correctly.

Overall, a data dictionary provides a strong place and location for individuals and an organization to pull data accurately. Hopefully, this allows organizations to not run into the problem the individual and organization did in my prior life. By using a data dictionary to mitigate risk or provide transparency to data, organizations are empowering a common language to be spoken around data.

Reading data and data fluency strategy

Now that we have looked at reading data and data fluency, the question can become: how do we do this? What kind of strategy should we employ to implement better work with reading data and speaking the language of data? Like other areas of data and analytical strategy, the answer lies in simplicity.

For data and analytical strategy to succeed and bring strong return on investment, it must tie back to the organization's goals and objectives. Unfortunately, a lot of times it doesn't work out this way. Far too often, the data and analytical strategy is separate from the business strategy. Do not fall into this trap! Ensure they tie together, with the data and analytical strategy used as a tool to help the business strategy to succeed. One aspect of the data and analytical strategy needs to be that of data literacy, with parts tied back to reading data and data fluency.

With reading data and data fluency, there will be commonalities and standard learning throughout an organization, but it is not a one-size-fits-all. For data literacy learning, such as reading data and data fluency, to succeed, we need to understand the skills and comfort of the individuals who are tasked with developing these skills. Assessing everyone's comfort and skill allows an organization to understand what steps and learning need to take place. Once the assessment is complete, utilizing individuals' different assessment scores, each participant can then proceed to learn how to read data better. Then, they can learn how to speak the language of data more effectively. This should enable organizations to avoid confusion and succeed more with data.

Organizational example

Bringing context and understanding to how the language of data will help an organization succeed with data and analytics can help all of us to see the flow of data through an organization. For our example, let's use an organization looking to study and understand the market for a new product launch. To begin, we will be studying the high-level flow from product ideation down to product launch.

Within your organization, the executive team has been looking at launching a new product into the world. Where did it come up with this new product? Through surveys, gathering market data, and studying competitors, the organization determined it had the data to understand the market and saw a new product was needed. To help with this, the team was tasked with analyzing all this data and information, and was able to find key indicators and trends, allowing the executives to make smart, intelligent decision. This is our first step of reading data and data fluency or communicating with data. Some of us may not notice it, but there are multiple instances.

The first area to examine is that of reading data by the team assigned to understand the market and what type of product would be available to help any gaps. Through the analysis and reading of the data, the team was able to decipher multiple gaps within the industry and regions under the microscope. This ability to read the data properly allowed the analysts and team to understand the market correctly. From there, the team needed to present the information and data effectively to the executive team. Here we can see the data fluency piece coming into play strongly. If the team of analysts and/or executive cannot share their thoughts or listen effectively, would the executives be able to understand the information to make a smarter decision? Here, we can clearly see how the flow of data and information needs to be read effectively and communicated the same.

Once the executive team has approved of the new product, it must communicate the desire to the appropriate teams to make this product. Is this data? Absolutely! We need to understand that data is not just numbers, but is also information that can be passed between the teams. The executive team and the analysts will need to communicate the appropriate information to the team building the product. The product team will need to be able to understand the data and information shared with them, being able to not only read the data and information in front of them, but also communicating with other parts of the organization as the product continues its progress.

Are we starting to see this free flow of data and information is not a small piece of a business's goals and objectives being met? The example we are covering is just a small one, hypothetical even, but we can clearly see how reading data and the ability to speak the language of data can help the organization achieve its goals and objectives. There are many aspects of where this can be put into place:

- Imagine an automobile company looking to roll out a new line of vehicles. The ability to read the information, data, and market will be critical to the right release and timing of the new vehicles.

- Think about all the streaming services we are now able to choose from, from Netflix to Hulu and more. Within these services, the ability to launch new channels or movies, the ability to build predictive models on what the audience will want, or the ability to run modeling to see preferences all can hinge on the organization's ability to read data and communicate it effectively.

- Think about our hospitals and healthcare systems, particularly when we are dealing with crises or other issues. The ability of hospitals to maintain a strong understanding of beds in use, operative care, and more can hinge on the ability to understand and read the data coming through, plus communicating effectively with individuals, cities, and in some cases entire countries.

- Finally, think about a government's ability to respond to the ebbs and flows of disasters, economies, pandemics, and more. The ability to properly read data and communicate effectively with a group of citizens or populations is key. This is also an essence of data literacy for individuals, because we want citizens to be data literate so they can truly understand and move forward with a government's goals and directives.

Chapter summary

Overall, data literacy has four characteristics: the ability to read, work with, analyze, and communicate with data. The ability to read and understand data may be the one that gets it all started, as how can one work with it, analyze, and finally communicate if they cannot read it? In this chapter we covered some important points around the world of reading data and then speaking the language of data. As we progress through further chapters, you will see how reading and speaking the language of data will become a more important part of the data literacy world.

Notes

1 Kopanakis, J (undated) 5 Real-World Examples of How Brands are Using Big Data Analytics [Blog], Mentionlytics. Available from: https://www.mentionlytics. com/blog/5-real-world-examples-of-how-brands-are-using-big-data-analytics/ (archived at https://perma.cc/4RKM-UJEF)

2 Suzor, T (2019) The Future of the Fan Experience at the US Open [Blog], IBM, 27 August. Available from: https://www.ibm.com/blogs/watson/2019/08/the-future-of-the-fan-experience-at-the-us-open/ (archived at https://perma.cc/64Z4-55AZ)

3 Marr, B (undated) Coca-Cola: Driving Success with AI and Big Data, Bernard Marr & Co. Available from: https://www.bernardmarr.com/default.asp?contentID=1280 (archived at https://perma.cc/P2ZX-NA49)

4 Kahn, Y (2019) These Are the Top 10 Brands in the World in 2019. Facebook Isn't One of Them, Business Insider, 18 October. Available from: https://markets.businessinsider.com/news/stocks/interbrand-top-10-brands-in-the-world-2019-10-1028610273 (archived at https://perma.cc/65FM-DGM2)

5 U.S. Department of Agriculture, Definition of Data Dictionary. Available from: https://data.nal.usda.gov/data-dictionary-purpose (archived at https://perma.cc/KYA7-AKE5)

06

Combining data literacy and the four levels of analytics

In an earlier chapter, we had the opportunity to jump into the four levels of analytics, sometimes called the four levels of analysis. To help jog our memories, the four levels of analytics are descriptive, diagnostic, predictive, and prescriptive. These four levels, when put into a holistic plan and approach to data and analytics work, help an organization to achieve its overall potential, not to mention return on investment for the dollars spent on these fields. The question can then be asked: how does data literacy pertain to the four levels of analytics? Turning back to our definition of data literacy, the ability to read, work with, analyze, and communicate with data, each one of the characteristics of data literacy plays an important and critical role in the four levels of analytics.

To help empower our knowledge and understanding of the four levels of analytics and data literacy, we will be dissecting each level of analytics and tying it to the four characteristics of analytics. To do this, we will be using examples to bring to light the overall power of these levels.

Data literacy and descriptive analytics

If you recall, the first level of analytics is descriptive analytics. In short, this is our observational analytics. This is where we can gain a knowledge and understanding, mainly looking backward at what has happened. This is a crucial aspect of an organization. Organizations need to know what happened in the past to help plan for the future, understand how sales trends are falling, understand how marketing campaigns performed, and a myriad of other reasons. How can data literacy play a part within this world of descriptive analytics?

The first characteristic of data literacy is reading data. I think this piece would be pretty straightforward. With descriptive analytics, whether you are viewing a dashboard, data visualization, or report, you must have the ability to comprehend the information presented to you. For example, take a look at this visualization of the London Underground from 1908 (Figure 6.1); what do you see? We can see different patterns of the rail lines, the different colors representing those lines, and the stops on the rails. Did you catch that? Overall, this visualization is pretty straightforward and easy to read. Reading the data and information presented, one can have an easy time understanding their way through the system.

FIGURE 6.1 London Underground Railways map, 1908

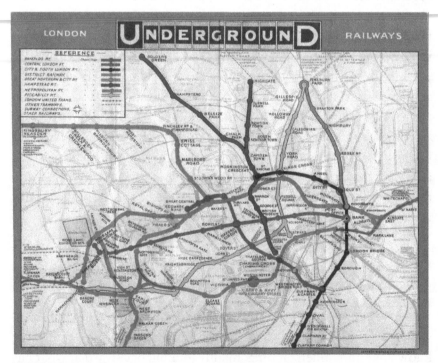

SOURCE Unknown author

Let's take a look at another example: hypothetical US Government spending (Figure 6.2). In this example, we can read the data and information presented to us. Can you tell which area of the Government had the biggest spend? What about income security?

Overall, both examples of descriptive analytics are easy to read because of the strong way the data visualizations are built. Remember, to read data is the ability to look at it and comprehend what is placed in front of us. This could be a data visualization, year-end report, PowerPoint presentation, and so forth. We need to ensure we are empowering individuals and organizations, through data literacy, for individuals to be able to read the descriptive analytics as they are presented to them.

Note: we won't be tackling in this book the myriads of ways a data visualization or reporting can go south, as those are tackled in other books, such as Ben Jones' *Avoiding Data Pitfalls*, or *The Big Book of Dashboards* by Andy Cotgreave, Jeffrey Shaffer, and Steve Wexler. Our purpose is to help us understand the importance of reading descriptive analytics.

The second characteristic of data literacy is of course working with data. Descriptive analytics and working with data go hand in hand, especially when working with data entails working with data visualizations, but there are other ways you may be working with data that you don't even realize. Have you ever had a month-end or year-end report in your hands, looking at budget and revenue numbers? Have you ever had a report on your computer screen that shares with you the click-through rate of a marketing campaign? Have you ever watched a PowerPoint presentation that had a chart or two in it? These are all ways an individual can work with data that is a descriptive analytic.

As for descriptive analytics, working with data can take on different meanings for different roles within an organization. We all know organizations are made up of many different roles, positions, and responsibilities. For some, working with data may just be handling the PowerPoint presentation or seeing the dashboard. For others, it will be their jobs to build and create the descriptive analytics. Yet others will be there giving directions on what kind of descriptive analytic is needed by the business (here is a tiptoe into communicating with data, in this case communicating what you need from the data).

FIGURE 6.2 Hypothetical US Government spending

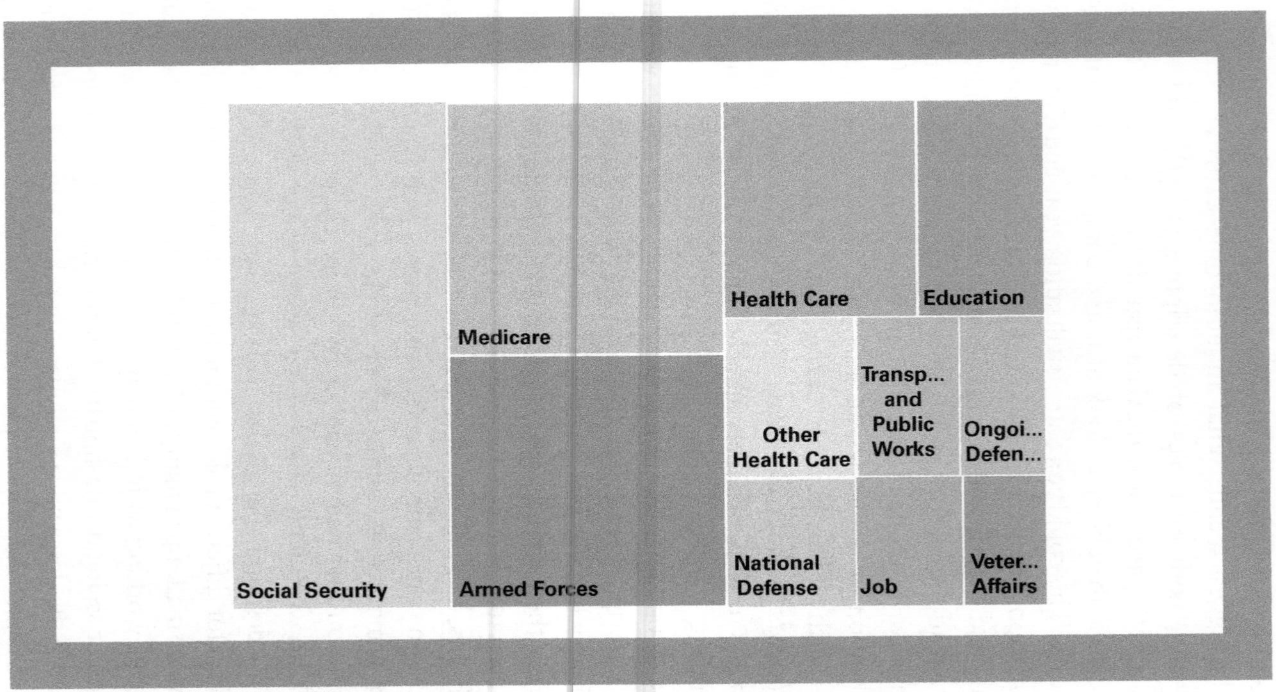

Overall, working with data takes on many faces as an organization deals with descriptive analytics. For each person, it is up to them and the organization to designate and understand a person's comfort and confidence with data literacy as to how to empower an individual with these skills.

The third characteristic of data literacy is analyzing data. For observational analytics, analyzing data is pretty straightforward: it is observing the point, trends, and the 'what is happening' of the data in front of you. For example, if you were presented with the line chart in Figure 6.3, could you tell me what the trend is for wolves, lions, and sharks? For two of them, the wolves and lions, it is pretty clear that wolf wildlife population is on the upswing, whereas the lions are on the downswing. What about the sharks? It looks to be sort of flat over the years.

Here we have analyzed and made observations of the data. The key here is we have only made observations of the data, we haven't determined 'why' the lines look the way they do. We only know what they do (stay tuned for the 'why' when we discuss data literacy and diagnostic analytics).

Finally, the last characteristic of data literacy is communicating with data. Here, the characteristic of communicating data may seem simple, but in some cases communicating with data is not a simple task. Unfortunately, speaking the language of data or data fluency isn't always that simple (although we wish it were). As such, when it comes to descriptive analytics, we need to ensure our communication is simple, concise, and effective. For example, looking at Figure 6.3 again, we could communicate the following: 'Our observations show that from 1990 to 1997 the wildlife population of wolves increased, while the wildlife population of lions decreased. The population of sharks bounced back and forth.' We should be careful in our dialogue to not make it seem like we can tell them 'why' it is happening, but just the observations we have seen.

When communicating with descriptive analytics, we also don't need flowery language or thoughts. We can keep it simple and to the point. As was discussed in the previous chapter, we want to create a common data dictionary and share with others important descriptive analytics, but use language that is easy to understand and common.

FIGURE 6.3   Animal population example

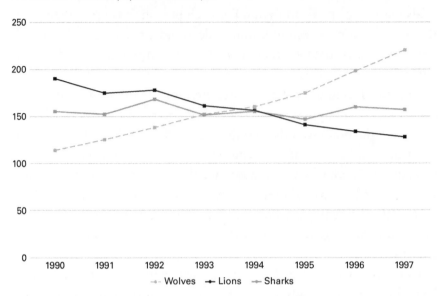

Overall, descriptive analytics is pretty straightforward within the world of data literacy. There are many things that can be done in descriptive analytics with data literacy, and it is up to the organization and individuals in the organization to ensure they are practicing and improving their data literacy skills so descriptive analytics can achieve efficacy and success.

Data literacy and diagnostic analytics

The second level of the four levels of analytics is diagnostic analytics; it is what I like to call the 'why' level of analytics. As we noted, descriptive analytics is observational analytics. It is observing what is happening, but it isn't telling us why it is happening. In steps the second level of analytics. This level of analytics is the essence of data literacy. Being able to find out why things happen allows an organization to truly drive insight, and insight can help drive answers and decisions for the organization. If you think about it, we can make observations, but it is when we dig in with our skills and abilities in data literacy where the insight, or 'why', is made apparent. Let's jump in to see how data literacy couples so nicely with diagnostic analytics.

To begin, reading data is the first step of the diagnostic analytical journey. As the first characteristic of data literacy, reading data means the ability to look at the data and information that is presented to you and comprehend it. This is of the utmost importance if one is to diagnose the data and information. Reading the data and information presented to someone in a descriptive analytic is vitally important for success in understanding why it happened. Reading data also enhances and enables an individual to ask more questions, ask for more data, and analyze more information.

The second characteristic of data literacy is working with data. Working with data can be a great way to dig into a descriptive analytic and find out the 'why' behind. Thanks to many business intelligence and analytics companies like Alteryx, Qlik, Tableau, and others, there are great tools that not only will build powerful visualizations and analyses, they will allow you to dig into the data, and manipulate it. Figure 6.4 is an example of a Qlik Sense dashboard.

Notice the filtering capability this dashboard provides. Now, does filtering allow us to find the insight that quickly? Well, maybe, but maybe not. Overall, filtering allows us to dig in more and more to find the insight.

For diagnostic analytics, working with data can pertain to the role again and here are a few examples:

- Executives: The executive team can play a vital role in diagnosing the 'why' within the data. Executives bring years of experience to the table when reports, dashboards, and other pieces of information are shown. Executives can ask questions, bring ideas to the table, and help spur on further conversation. The key for them may be communicating to those with the technical skills and abilities on what they think is happening, and then request further investigation.

- Data analyst: The data analyst is empowered with data through the democratization of data and putting it in their hands. The data analyst may be the one working with the data to both build a data visualization and then filtering and manipulating it to see what is happening with the descriptive analytic.

- Data scientist: A data scientist can work with data intensely to find out the why behind things. Then, with the why, and we will discuss this more in the third level of analytics, make predictions and design models.

Of course, these are not all of the position types in an organization; there are many, but working with data will take on many forms within diagnostic analytics.

The third characteristic within data literacy is analyzing data and, in this case, maybe it is a bit redundant. Analyzing data is the essence of diagnostic analytics. Let's take the example of a doctor. A doctor will look to help and diagnose a patient. First, they are looking at descriptive signals, such as what symptoms a person is experience, what outward symptoms are presenting themselves, and so forth. Then, the doctor will use their experience and skill to build a case on what the diagnoses is. One thing the doctor does to diagnose properly is they turn to their skills, knowledge, and learning. With that knowledge and learning, the doctor can work towards figuring out what is happening.

The same needs to happen with a workforce. First, they might not all have the background to diagnose the analytic, but they should be developing their data literacy skills to ensure correct and proper 'whys'. This working with data is a powerful way for an individual to contribute effectively to the world of insights, and these insights are what can be used to empower an organization with decisions.

Finally, again, the last characteristic of data literacy is communicating with data. Here, the characteristic of communicating data is

FIGURE 6.4 Qlik filtering example

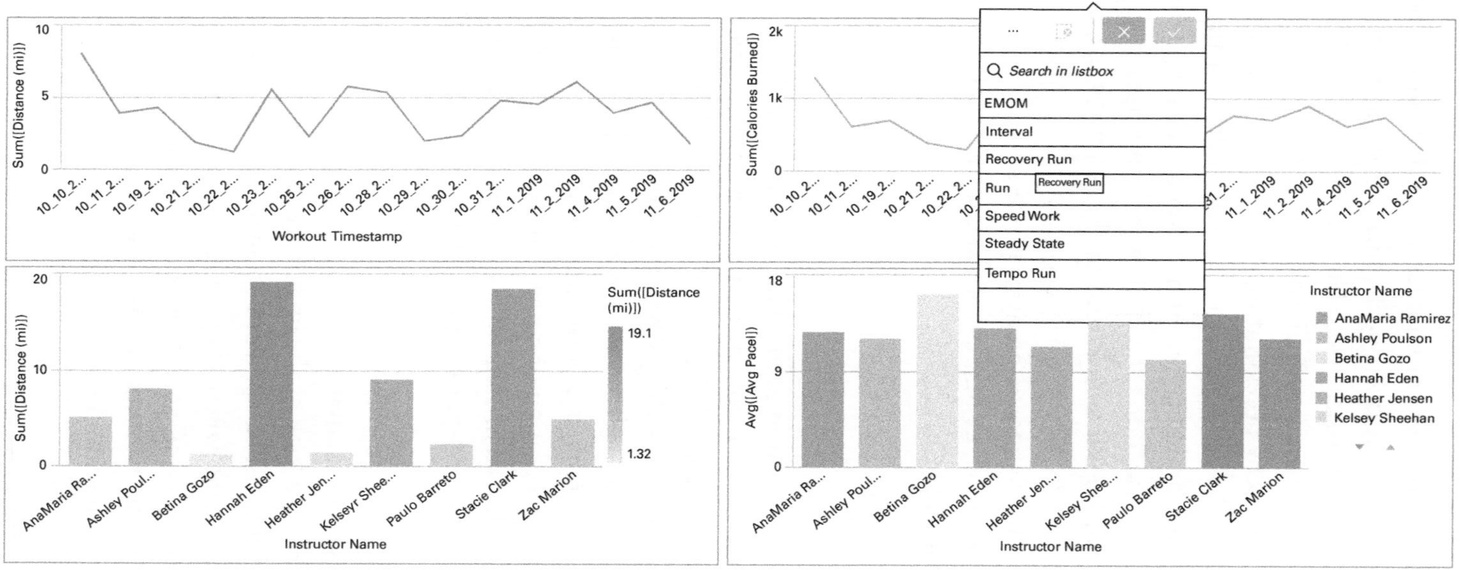

essential, as the proper communication of insight can help drive the decision. If communicated poorly, then the decision the organization may make can be drastically off. Unfortunately, speaking the language of data or data fluency isn't always efficient or effective in the world of analytics, thereby necessitating data literacy learning. Again, as in descriptive analytics, diagnostic analytics takes on the same needs: simple, concise, and effective. When communicating with diagnostic analytics, we also don't need flowery language, but to-the-point work. We can keep it simple and to the point. Utilize common data fluency to create the proper communication plan and strength throughout the diagnostic analysis process.

What are some examples of diagnostic analytics in action? I thought you would never ask.

Example 1

One of the best examples of using descriptive and diagnostic analytics was given to us through the London cholera epidemic of 1854, discussed in Chapter 4 (Figure 6.5). The legend goes (and I stress the word legend here, as things become more widespread and fanciful overtime) that through a data visualization, John Snow helped with the cholera outbreak and prevented a new outbreak. While, yes, it did help with the prevention of a new outbreak, what the data visualization did was show and confirm some theories that were going around about the water pump. One thing the visualization did do was help to change the way cholera was viewed, as it was thought to travel through the air. Let's jump into this visualization to understand the first two levels of analytics.

First, when we look at the image, let's understand what it is showing. John Snow asked someone to map out the cases of the cholera outbreak, showing where they were occurring. As can be seen in the visualization, we can see a large cluster of cases around Broad Street, in particular the water pump. We also see cases up and down Broad Street, where the pump was located.

FIGURE 6.5   John Snow's cholera visualization, 1854

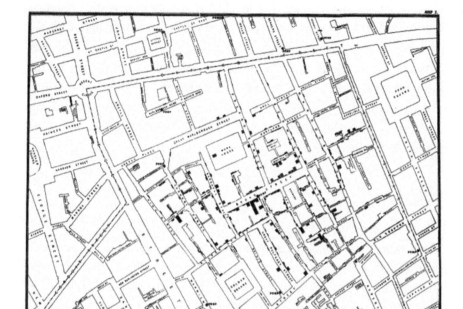

Essentially what I just did was descriptive analytics. I was able to give a description of the area and what is happening. Further analysis would show different things occurring, but we are looking directly at the descriptive analytic at this time (you are more than free to conduct more analysis around the different aspects of the map, such as the brewery; it is theorized that the brewery didn't have cases as those people were given free alcohol and didn't drink water).

For us, as we move through the analytical levels, we can see that the descriptive analysis can spur on more questions. If we are looking at the descriptive analytic itself, we could start to wonder in our mind: why do we see this big cluster around the Broad Street pump? In particular, to the left we can see a large number of cholera cases. In fact, we see many cases running up and down Broad Street, so why are we not seeing as many cases going down the side streets? By asking questions, we can dig into the second level of analytics: diagnostic analytics.

Once we have this data visualization of cholera in front of us, we are now diving through the overall process of diagnostic analytics. With the bundling of cases around the pump, we can start asking questions about the pump or characteristics of Broad Street that can lead us to the pump. It was found that, yes, the water was contaminated and spreading the disease. It is said that John Snow helped change data journalism.[1]

Example 2

For this example, let's turn to the sales industry. Across industries, salespeople look to market their products, create leads, and drive revenue. How can the world of descriptive and diagnostic analytics help a sales team or person succeed in their roles? When we go through this example, you will see that descriptive and diagnostic analytics are both powerful ways to drive sales leads in an organization. To start, let's look at how *descriptive analytics* plays a part to help shape and tell the story of what sales leads are looking like in their organization, how the customers look within different demographics, and how numbers are trending against forecasts.

- The first example is what sales leads look like within an organization. Utilizing the power of analytical software, such as a business intelligence tool like Qlik or Tableau, the organization can pour sales lead data into the data visualization tools. From there an organization can filter and dive into building a strong picture of what sales leads look like within the organization, whether by the size of the opportunity, the location of the lead to divert it to the right sales rep, or look at a different industry to also help the shaping of which the sales rep will be taking the lead. As you can imagine, by being able to use descriptive analytics, the organization can shape the story of the sales leads.

- The second example is the demographic breakdown of customers. As you can imagine, the ability to visually see the breakdown of your customers by location, years as customer, annual revenue spend, and so many more metrics can truly empower a sales person to understand the picture of the organization.

- Finally, looking at the trends of the actual sales coming against forecast is vitally important. Without the ability of an organization to break down what is happening with forecasted numbers against actual numbers, the organization can miss the mark on setting targets for sales representatives, and overall not have a strong picture of what is happening in the sales organization. We do need to understand, though, that this is still just the descriptive analytic and painting the picture of what sales looks like against the forecast. We need to dig into the diagnostic side of all these examples.

As we work through the analytical chain, we move from descriptive to *diagnostic analytics* on the sales side of the organization.

- In our first example, the sales representative was looking at the different sales leads within the organization. Through the sales rep's data literacy skills, they can look at the sales leads, read the data presented to them, and figure out which company or sales lead might be more beneficial than another. This is a powerful skill to possess. Because the sales rep can read the information presented to them on the sales lead, they can then work with the data and analyze it to plan out how they will attack these sales leads.

- The second example was understanding the different breakdown and layout of the customers through demographic information. Just looking at the breakdown in a descriptive analytic will not paint the entire picture of the different customers the sales rep has, but by digging further into the information to find out why customers spend what they do, and purchase the products they do, the sales rep can understand how to target these customers better and, maybe more importantly, work to establish better relationships with the customers because they have developed a better understanding of who the customer is beyond the descriptive analytic.

- Finally, the example of understanding the trends of actual sales revenue coming in versus the forecast can be vital for a sales rep looking to make their monthly quota. As a sales rep studies the trends, whether they are doing better than forecast or worse, the rep must move beyond the descriptive analytic that is the trend line and actual numbers, and dig into 'why' they are doing better or worse. Doing so can be a vital skill and action on a regular basis that sets the tone for the sales rep in making their monthly and quarterly figures. This will also allow the organization to better plan for future forecasts and trends.

Overall, as can be seen in the cholera and sales team examples, the ability to make observational analytics with descriptive analytics, and then transitioning the observation into the 'why' or insight, can help drive power within an organization. By developing data literacy skills in reading the data, working with it, analyzing it for insight, and then, finally, communicating what is found is crucial. We cannot forget this last step: communicating what is found. Can you imagine if John Snow hadn't communicated ideas, theories, or findings regarding the water pump on Broad Street, what would have happened with the outbreak? With our sales reps, can you imagine if they found something in the sales leads and didn't share it? Can you imagine if the sales rep found out something with the demographics that showed a direct impact of 'why' on the sales forecast, but then withheld the information, how much trouble they would be in? The fourth characteristic of data literacy is communicating with data. This skill has to also be worked on and improved within descriptive and diagnostic analytics. In reality, all four characteristics of data literacy are powerful in helping individuals handle and navigate the worlds of descriptive and diagnostic analytics.

Data literacy and predictive analytics

The third level of analytics is, of course, *predictive analytics*. Predictive analytics and data literacy – how do they go together? In reality, not everyone needs to have technical skills, so what does data literacy have to do with predictive analytics? Unfortunately, because the world of predictive (and the next level, prescriptive) analytics can involve technical skills, such as coding or statistics, the need for everyone to be involved with predictive analytics can be overlooked. This mentality will hurt overall data and analytical work. Data literacy has a direct tie to predictive analytics – let's see how.

First, data literacy has a very key skill that is necessary: reading data. In the case of predictive analytics, each time a predictive model is finished or the analysis run, we need people to be able to read the results. By being able to read the results, the individual confident in their data literacy skills can understand and then make a decision. The end game of data literacy is to make smarter decisions with data.

Second, data literacy is directly tied with data fluency, the ability to speak the language of data. I want you to imagine to yourself you work in your marketing organization and you really want to dig into the data of a new marketing campaign (this is the third characteristic of data literacy: analyze). The problem is the data is very complex, so you need to turn to someone who can process the data and dig into it deeper than the descriptive level. As you try to understand the data and information in front of you, to diagnose the descriptive analytic, you need help. By being confident in your data literacy skills, you have the ability to communicate effectively what it is you are trying to do. You have the ability to share your ideas, thoughts, and things you need, and can work with the technical group to get your analysis complete. Do you see how these four levels of analytics work holistically?

To help us understand this world of predictive analytics more, let us look at some examples of predictive analytics and how it applies to data literacy.

Example 1: Meteorology and predicting the weather

How many of us like to know what the weather is going to be? How many of us use a weather app on our phones to ensure that we are dressed appropriately? I know that I for sure use a weather app or website when I am traveling for work. I once traveled to Finland at the end of November for some data literacy work. Finland at the end of November is not warm. I may not have brought the right coat, but I did need to understand the weather to pack for the overseas trip. This is something I do on a regular basis when I travel. I am sure a lot of people do. Do you realize how much work is built into the predictive modeling for weather? I will not put much detail in this book, Nate Silver did a good job of sharing the power of modeling in weather in his book *The Signal and the Noise: Why So Many Predictions Fail – but Some Don't*, but the weather presents a unique challenge.

First, the weather is a very complex system and there have been vast improvements in how it is modeled and predictive analytics built. Through this complexity, those skilled in building the predictive analytics now need to communicate it to the audience; the audience being us. Then, once communicated to us, we, those confident in understanding the predictions, can make a decision about the weather. Here, again, we see descriptive analytics in place (the forecast), diagnostic analytics in place (why the weather will be what it is), and predictive analytics being modeled (predicting the forecast forward). We are also seeing data literacy working in place: reading the data (both those modeling the data and those reading the forecast to make a decision), working with data from those building the models and those handling it, analyzing it on the technical side, and then having it communicated out to the audience.

Example 2: Sports

If there is one industry where prediction is commonplace, it is the sporting world. Think of the last time you were following a sport, if you follow sports. Who was predicted to win the game you were following? Did they have predictions on the number of soccer or football goals your favorite player would score? Did they predict which the top teams will be on the season (maybe a better question is, are they ever right)? Sport has so many complexities and realities that modeling and predictive analytics is a powerful way for teams, players, and franchises to look to excel and win the matches and games they want to play. I want to get more specific on the predictive analytics with sports.

The National Basketball Association in the United States has embraced predictive analytics in different ways. It is described in an article by Martijn Hosten: 'In the NBA, the most popular basketball competition, they also embraced AI and predictive analytics in their coaching strategies. For example, models are able to predict whether a player that is in a certain position will either try to score or pass (and to whom).'[2] If the NBA has embraced strategic thinking with predictive modeling around coaching strategies, think about all sports and what possibilities exist with predictive modeling.

There is absolutely a catch here: what if those building models were poor at communicating what they had found. Would that work well? Of course the answer is no. This shows us that we need to help those who are technically sound in data and analytics to communicate effectively what they find, we need the coaches and players having enough data literacy confidence to understand what the predictions show, and we need a holistic approach and strategy to succeed.

Example 3: Targeted marketing campaigns

The final example is one straight from the business world: who should we target with our marketing campaign? Organizations are trying to improve, understand, and find better ways to target their customers. Through this, predictive analytics can empower the organization. This example of targeted marketing can really bring to light the predictive analytics power for targeted approaches. Please note that these predictive analytics for a targeted campaign would need to ensure they are not biased or discriminatory. Through the power of a true holistic strategy, we can see how data literacy really plays through the organizational work of data and analytical strategy, and predictive analytics.

When a marketing organization is looking to take the targeted approach, the analysts or data scientists building the predictive modeling will need to gather the data. Through this data gathering, and with a clear understanding of the communicated desire and goal, the analysts or data scientists can work to build models and analysis around the targeted approach. Once the model and results are built, the individual or team can communicate the results to the marketing group, which is confident in its data literacy and can understand how to implement. Then, they can strike with the campaign. Then, as results from the campaign start to come in, the group can start a reiterative process of analyzing the predictive work.

Overall, through all three of these examples, we can see that predictive modeling plays a significant part with data literacy. We see that people need to be able to read the results, work with the models and data, analyze the information, and communicate effectively.

Data literacy and prescriptive analytics

When we think of prescriptive analytics, we need to start thinking more technically, but please note, it is not all technical and shouldn't be viewed as such. You might ask: I thought data literacy was not technical, what is happening here? That is correct! Data literacy is not the technical side, but remember the topic of data fluency and this ability to speak the language of data? When individuals are working through data and analytical work, and are employing data literacy skills, it is then incumbent on them to be comfortable understanding or reading the data and information that comes from prescriptive analytics, plus it is then important to be able to communicate effectively with others any decisions and insight that is found. With that said, just what is prescriptive analytics?

One definition of prescriptive analytics comes to us from an article by the company Talend and states:

> Prescriptive analytics is a process that analyzes data and provides
> instant recommendations on how to optimize business practices to suit
> multiple predicted outcomes. In essence, prescriptive analytics takes
> the 'what we know' (data), comprehensively understands that data to
> predict what could happen, and suggests the best steps forward based
> on informed simulations.[3]

Later in the article we are taught that prescriptive analytics utilizes similar modeling structures to predict outcomes and then utilizes a combination of machine learning, business rules, artificial intelligence, and algorithms to simulate various approaches to these numerous outcomes. It then suggests the best possible actions to optimize business practices. It is the 'what should happen'. With these definitions, we can see where the technical and non-technical can combine.

First, the technical. Within data and analytics, there are terms that are thrown around and could be considered 'buzz worthy': machine learning and artificial intelligence. Here, within prescriptive analytics, we can see the need for the technical employees. These employees possess skills within coding, data science, statistics, and work with the data and technology. With artificial intelligence and machine learning doing the work for the human side (we will not dive into these topics within this book, as there are a myriad of books in the world covering these vast and important topics), second, we need the humans on the results end of the equation, able to interpret, implement, and ensure the decisions are strong. Some real-world examples can help us to understand prescriptive analytics.

Example 1: Medical diagnosis

In the field of medicine, the power of machine learning and artificial intelligence is expanding, empowering, and helping make medicine more effective. Imagine you are a doctor and sitting next to you is a computer, taking in a patient's vast medical history, along with symptoms, current health, etc. You, as the doctor, want to provide this patient with the greatest care you can; and by utilizing the vast amounts of data and work that machine learning, artificial intelligence, e.g. prescriptive analytics, can provide, you are able to more efficiently and effectively diagnose the patient and give prescriptive care. Imagine you are a doctor where machine learning and artificial intelligence are there to help you diagnose a certain cancer type well before it was meted out in an image. Imagine utilizing machine learning and artificial intelligence to help create cures for diseases. The medical field truly is one that can be and is being transformed through the power of data.

One may ask: what about the naysayers that are present in this field – the doctors, nurses, and administrators who don't want to take this route? The world of medicine, and science for that matter, is one that is constantly evolving. One common practice of medicine was blood letting, where an individual would have blood drained to help them get better (yes, this is a very simplified version, but to learn more, you can go study or read up on the practice), and this practice went on for at least 3,000 years.[4] With this information, and from the same referenced article, we learn that blood letting only stopped in the late 19th century. That is relatively recent. If it wasn't for change and more information (data if you will) coming into existence, we still might be blood letting today. Now, I don't know about you, but I am sure glad that to cure me of certain ailments, they aren't just draining my blood and hoping for success.

Example 2: Product sales

This second example is one, I feel, that should go without saying: product sales. If we are to take a look at companies who are looking to sell product, find which products customers want, and so forth, what do you think the power of prescriptive analytics could do for them? If the answer is a whole lot, you would be correct.

Let's take a look at some of our favorite companies (well, some of the most popular might be a better way to say it). Imagine for me that you work in data and analytics for Coca-Cola. Coca-Cola is one of the most recognizable brands and frequently ranks in the top 10 brands in the world. Coca-Cola is a company that understands data. In your role, your job is to find the most popular flavors of soda, where they sell the greatest, and where you should start to target brands to uplift sales. Do you personally want to sift through all of the data, or would having a machine that can learn much faster than you (yes, I am sorry, but they can) or artificial intelligence dissect the data and help you find the right course of action? I am personally going to choose the machine learning and artificial intelligence. Now, does that mean these two areas always get it right? Of course not! But, we are in a position of data literacy where we can reiterate and strengthen our plans.

Another company that can benefit greatly from prescriptive analytics is the Ford Motor Company (and knowing the work Ford does in data and analytics, I know it is in good shape). What kind of car or truck should Ford be making, based off all the information and data it possesses? What kind of features should be included? Maybe the most important: how will these features and changes impact safety measures? Utilizing prescriptive analytics, the organization has the power to work through complex data and models, utilizing prescriptive analytics to analyze the various possible outcomes, and with a strong, confident, data literate workforce, decisions and iteration can be made.

The final company we will look at is one of my personal favorites: Disney. It isn't that often that Disney doesn't succeed with its launches, parks, movies, and products. What if Disney had the power of machine learning and artificial intelligence to understand the popularity of products, what movie it should make next, and how to staff and ensure its theme park visitors are happy? Well, Disney does an excellent job with its strategy and work; the utilization of machine learning and artificial intelligence is an amazing tool in its arsenal of success driving work.

Overall, prescriptive analytics has power. The ability of machines to do some intense heavy lifting on data can free up a workforce to truly succeed with data and analytics, but herein lies the direct tie to data literacy: if the workforce is not comfortable and confident with data literacy, is the organization going to have as much success?

Data literacy and the four levels of analytics – the holistic puzzle

As we have marched through this chapter, you can probably tell how powerful data literacy is in the success of the four levels of analytics. The ability of an individual to read, work with, analyze, and communicate using data touches upon what I like to call the holistic puzzle of analytics. If organizations are stuck at any of these levels, then we are not getting this sound overall strategy. The ability to read data enables us to make observations to understand what is happening, and allows us to understand predictions and outcomes. Working with data allows us to manipulate the information and data presented, to dig in and filter, change, and create new perspectives on the information. This is quite empowering and could unlock the direct insight that is needed to find the 'why' of diagnostic analytics. The ability to analyze the data in front of us comes from reading and understanding the data, working with it at times to give that variation, and to dig in. Because we need to see the whole picture, this is a part of all the levels of analytics. Finally, the ability to communicate delves throughout all the levels, as we need to communicate the observation, insight, prediction, and various outcomes. In doing so, the holistic puzzle can succeed.

Chapter summary

To conclude this chapter, we need to ensure we really drive home the point of the power of the four levels of analytics and data literacy. These two areas can be overlooked when it comes to the millions and millions of dollars companies are spending on data and analytic success. The reality is, when an organization is implementing data and analytical work, not having a sound understanding of what the four levels of analytics consist of will hamper success. We can see this in organizations around the world that are not getting their desired return on investment in data. Second, data literacy is needed to ensure the organization can implement the four levels of analytics successfully. If individuals are not comfortable and confident with data literacy, we cannot expect them to truly succeed with work within the four levels of analytics, nor with work that helps to drive the holistic puzzle that is found therein.

With these pieces in mind, it becomes even more important that a sound strategy is in place for learning, adopting, and building these programs, but how can an organization do this without an overall sound data and analytical strategy? In the next chapter, we find out just what a strong data and analytical strategy is and how data literacy plays a part. In particular, we will work through a workforce to understand how different roles play a different part within the work. Some roles we will cover are the executive suite, decision-makers, team leaders, analysts versus data science, and individual contributors. Remember the data literacy umbrella in Figure 4.1? In Chapter 4 we covered certain areas that this umbrella captures, but how do the different roles play a part? We will dig in through data literacy and strategy.

Notes

1 Rogers, S (2013) John Snow's Data Journalism: The Cholera Map that Changed the World, *The Guardian*, 15 March. Available from: https://www.theguardian.com/news/datablog/2013/mar/15/john-snow-cholera-map (archived at https://perma.cc/435J-ZBJW)

2 Hosten, M (2017) Artificial Intelligence and Predictive Analytics in Sports: A Blessing for Some, a Nightmare for Others, We Are 4C, 4 September. Available from: https://weare4c.com/blog/2017-09-04-artificial-intelligence-and-predictive-analytics-in-sports-a-blessing-for-some-a-nightmare-for-others (archived at https://perma.cc/P5AE-R93U)

3 Talend (undated) What is Prescriptive Analytics? Talend. Available from: https://www.talend.com/resources/what-is-prescriptive-analytics/ (archived at https://perma.cc/DFV9-ANWF)

4 Greenstone, G (2010) The History of Bloodletting, *BC Medical Journal*, January and February. Available from: https://bcmj.org/premise/history-bloodletting (archived at https://perma.cc/3HJR-WYB3)

07

The steps of data literacy learning

So far, we have covered what data literacy is, and you may ask: what can I do to start learning data literacy, or how can I become more confident in my data literacy? I would like to assure you that going back to school to become a data scientist or to learn statistics is not necessary. Instead, there are plenty of opportunities in the market to learn more about data science or statistics. The reality is, and should be said over and over, that not everyone needs to be a data scientist or statistician, but everyone does need to be data literate.

In this chapter, we will cover data literacy learning strategies and what can be done by organizations to help individuals be more confident in these skills. We look at what an organization can do to build a solid and sound data literacy strategy, and how it can empower its workforce with the right kind of learning. We will also look at the four characteristics of the data literacy definition, ensuring you can walk away from reading this book with ideas around what you can do *today* to start improving.

For an organization to understand its data literacy learning, it must first understand its overall data and analytics strategy. Doing either of these independently will not benefit the company overall. In fact, by trying to build a data literacy strategy *without* knowing the organization's holistic data and analytics strategy would be like trying to train for a marathon but not knowing what a marathon actually is. For an organization to succeed with data and analytical learning, data literacy, the organization needs to:

- know and understand what it wants to do with data and analytics;
- understand how it wants to empower and help its employees and workforce succeed.

To help build this out, in this chapter we explore multiple areas of data and analytics from a learning perspective:

- the role of leadership and the executive team;
- the role of data and analytical strategy with data literacy learning;
- a data literacy learning framework and approach (hint: it is not a one-size-fits-all);
- learning for the four characteristics of data literacy;
- learning for a strong data literate culture;
- and, finally, other areas of focus for data literacy learning (such as data ethics).

Overall, learning within the world of data literacy is essential for individuals and organizations to truly succeed with data and analytics.

The role of leadership and data literacy learning

When it comes to data literacy learning, there is one key aspect to ensure the program and project works and is successful: the role of leadership. It's unlikely a project will succeed if you fail to secure the full buy-in from those in charge. If you do not have the buy-in of leadership, how successful do you think you will be in getting the right amount of money to run your project or program? I am guessing not very successful! You need the support of leadership from not only a program perspective but also a budget perspective. What are the main roles of leadership towards data literacy learning?

The first role that leadership plays in data literacy learning is the support and buy-in that is needed for a data literacy learning engagement to succeed. Have you ever in your career not jumped onboard with a new program and product because you knew that leadership did not financially back it or you didn't know exactly what was going to happen in the program or product? Now, let's turn that question around: have you ever been inspired by or followed a leader because you believed in them, the product they were producing, or the vision they were sharing? Leaders possess the power to attract followers. If a workforce does not see a leader buy-in to a data literacy program, why would they themselves buy-in? Leaders from the executive suite and decision-making framework need to show support for a program, drive the program throughout the company, and ensure they give proper and strong communication throughout an organization.

With that said, I do not want to belittle one key area of data literacy learning and program success that can be overlooked: the power of a grassroots movement. While it's crucial for an organization to have a leadership buy-in to drive data literacy learning within an organization, it is also immensely powerful for an organization to have a strong grassroots movement toward data literacy. As leaders try to share their data literacy vision and help empower a workforce with success, having a group of employees in the organization can also help drive support, initiative, and desire toward data literacy work which can be a critical step for data literacy learning. Then, this group of grassroots data literacy individuals can become internal data literacy evangelists for your program. Data and analytics truly are at the forefront of organizations' needs and desires, so leadership cannot take a passive tone when it comes to data literacy learning. It's important the leadership portray a strong message of support. If you are a leader in your organization, put enthusiasm and strength behind your words and desire to help empower your workforce with data literacy. Some people may perceive data and analytics as boring or intimidating subjects, which is why it's important to show enthusiasm so the team is more receptive to the benefits of becoming data literate. As a leader, you have the ability to set that tone in a powerful and efficacious way.

Along with the right tone and sentiment, leadership should also be willing to invest in the data literacy learning of the organization. In a study conducted by the business intelligence and analytics firm Qlik, it was found that 'despite 92 per cent of business decision-makers believing it is important for their employees to be data literate, only 17 per cent report that their business significantly encourages employees to become more confident in data'.[1] In other words, don't just talk the talk; you need to walk the walk – an organization must invest in its workforce properly.

I was once asked the question: do you invest first in the technology or in people? The answer seems obvious: the people. Unfortunately, for years, organizations have invested too much money in technology and data sourcing, software, etc., and the human element was simply forgotten. In reality, a strong partnership of learning between the human element *and* technology should be the answer. Leaders should ensure they are enthusiastically investing in their own data literacy learning so they can look to obtain a strong return on investment for their data and analytical investments.

The biggest roadblock and obstacle to data and analytical success is that of culture. If an organization's culture is not ready to absorb data analytical work, then the investments in the proper software, technology, and data are not necessarily going to work. The leadership team must ensure that it's investing in the right culture framework, structure, and empowerment so individuals and the organization can succeed properly with data and analytics. This culture needs to include the power and characteristics that can ensure success. We will explore the culture more in the learning aspect later in the chapter when we discuss individual learning.

The role of data and analytical strategy and data literacy learning

We will now explore how data and analytical strategy works together with data literacy learning. We will look at it from two angles:

1 What part of the data and analytical strategy deals with data literacy?

2 How does data literacy learning empower data and analytical success?

First, how does data literacy learning step in with data and analytical strategy? As organizations invest millions and millions of dollars into the world of data and analytics, a strong data and analytical strategy need to be in place so organizations see a return on the investments. As a part of a holistic, strong data and analytics strategy, there must be a strong element of learning and empowerment. Think of a data and analytical strategy as a machine that has certain levers that need to be pulled in order for the machine to produce the desired result. Each lever has a purpose and power. One of the levers needs to be proper learning, along with proper technology, data governance, sourcing, and the largest list (think of the data literacy umbrella). When these levers are pulled properly, the machine can run smoothly, but if not, the machine could produce something, but it probably won't look anything like the desired result. Ensure your organization has a holistic approach to data and analytical work, and this includes the learning and empowerment of the human element.

The second aspect of strategy that needs to be understood is that data literacy learning can help ensure a strong understanding of data and analytical strategy. In this case, we are almost dealing with a 'what comes first' scenario: the chicken or the egg, or in our case, the data literacy learning or the data and analytical strategy. In essence, we need to ensure we are creating both, to ensure the proper success with data and analytics. Ensure your organization is working hard to put in place a holistic strategy, capitalizing on the asset that is data, in addition to focusing on introducing suitable learning and frameworks on data. When you are learning about data, analytics, and so forth, guess what will happen with your strategy? You should see a direct tie to your strategy being a success, with its pieces becoming stronger and more effective, and stronger data-driven decisions being made. This is the holistic approach to data and analytical strategy and data literacy. Data literacy learning will empower an organization's workforce to understand the strategy, its power, and how to implement it effectively. Without strong data literacy learning, the strategy can fall flat on its face. I have been privy to many instances where organizations have not been as successful as they should have been because a holistic approach was not employed.

A data literacy learning framework and approach

In the introduction to this chapter, I hinted at something very important: data literacy learning, whether for an individual or an organization, should not be seen as a one-size-fits-all approach. There are some industries or fields where an approach to learning can be the same for everyone, where you get an out-of-the-box approach that is the same for each person that participates and takes the course. Data literacy is not that kind of field. For suitable learning to take place within the field and arena of data literacy, the learning should be more tailored and understood for each organization and individual. Let's take a look at a few different steps that can be implemented to see a data literacy initiative succeed.

Step 1: Understanding your data and analytical landscape and ownership

The first step to a proper data literacy learning strategy will be for those driving the data literacy initiative, which can be various groups in an organization (for example, human resources versus culture and talent versus the chief information officer's office), to understand the overall goals and strategic operations for the organization on the whole. Therefore, a solid, holistic approach to data and analytical work is not just needed – it is crucial. One may ask who owns the data literacy initiative? Is it one particular group?

This is a very good question and I wish there was an easy, one-click button solution and answer. The reality is that each organization is made up of and designed in a different manner, with different policies and procedures. These differences in policies, procedures, organizational structure, and so forth do not enable us to say: 'Data literacy must be owned by this group, run out of that group, and empowered in this area.' Just like data literacy is not a one-stop shop for learners and organizations, the same can be said about who owns the data literacy work and aspects. The key is to have executive or leadership buy-in, which we have discussed, and a solid plan. If your organization has a chief data officer, fantastic, look to maybe run it through that person. If your organization does not have a chief data or analytics officer, but all data and analytics are run through the chief information officer's office, then have the data literacy initiative run through that individual and group. The key is to have the initiative run through the upper echelons of the data and analytical ownership that exists in the organization.

When an organization sets up a data literacy initiative in this manner, it becomes easier for the organization to understand the data and analytical landscape, because the group who is most likely running data and analytical initiatives will now also be the one who is running the data literacy initiative. You will also have leadership buy-in through the initiative, as the person you are selecting should come from the executive team or high leadership of the organization.

Step 2: Understand your organizational skill set with data and analytics

Once an organization has a solid understanding of the ownership of data and analytical work, plus a sound understanding of the organization's data and analytical landscape and strategy, one can then turn to the second step: assessing the workforce. This is an absolute key to data literacy success!

As organizations look to implement the right data literacy strategy and what investments are necessary for success, it is key they start from the right foundation. When we think of a building or house, the right foundation is key for the sound structural integrity and longevity of the edifice. A similar type of approach is appropriate for data literacy plans and strategies. To do this, organizations should set out to dive in and understand the overall skill set that exists within the organization towards data and analytical work. This foundational understanding can be crucial for the organization to implement the right learning path and strategy.

One key element of this type of assessment should be to determine where your organization's skills gap exists and what areas of data and analytics need a closer, stronger inspection. There are different assessments that exist out there for this type of work: Qlik has a data literacy program, with its product agnostic approach, or Tableau with its

Tableau Blue Print, designed to help create a Tableau driven data culture. The key is to help assess where the gaps exist. If an organization can understand where its skills gap exists, then finding the right learning path and program to help fill in those gaps is the key.

Again, the key, strong element to a proper data literacy program is to understand and assess a workforce and organization. Without this element, the one-size-fits-all approach is easier to buy and implement, but will not get the specific, desired outcomes an organization is looking for.

Step 3: Set the proper data literacy strategy and program, with desired outcomes

After we understand the landscape of data and analytics at an organization, and once we have assessed the organization through a proper survey or assessment, it then becomes imperative to understand what kind of program to implement. This isn't rocket science and this is why it becomes so important an organization takes the time to survey and use assessments to implement this kind of strategy. The assessment should serve as a powerful roadmap for the organization to find, invest in, and then implement the right strategy. Without this assessment, how can we know whether the plan and implementation strategy we are using for our data literacy program and initiative are any good? If we do not assess the overall workforce how can we know success if we do not have a desired outcome?

This last question is also a key to data literacy learning and initiatives: *what is it we are trying to accomplish?* This goes along with understanding an organization's data and analytical landscape, that is, understanding an organization should arrive at the understanding of what it is trying to do with the investments it is making in data and analytics. With a sound understanding of the outcomes an organization is trying to succeed with, plus a strong understanding of the skill set of the organization (and, consequently, the skills gaps that exist), an organization is in a strong position to implement the right data literacy program.

To find a good program, organizations should invest the time, energy, and money to put in place the right plan. Just 'settling' for a program because it is cheap or less expensive, is not a good strategy. When we think of the power of data and analytical work, one thing this type of work can do for an organization is to save or gain money. Investing appropriately in the right program is an essential element to the work, as in the end, the right investment in the right data literacy program could reap a very large return for an organization.

Step 4: Conduct proper surveys and communications for feedback

When dealing with the world of data literacy learning, one key aspect we should emphasize is the power of a good feedback loop. To help us illuminate and understand the power of a feedback look, let me turn to a personal example that I utilize over and over: my training plans for an ultra-marathon.

In the world of ultra-marathons, maintaining proper fitness is imperative. Having the right diet and eating habits plus having a strong and solid training plan is key. Within that plan are lots of miles being run, and it should include good cross-training and stretching to ensure your body doesn't burn out or get injured during the program; oh, and let's not forget core work. There is one underlying element through it all that needs to be listened to: your body's feedback. As you train for such an intensive and grueling event, with ultra-marathons essentially starting at the 50 km distance and going up and above 200 miles (on feet, by the way), there can be many things going wrong. If you don't listen to your body's feedback on how the training is going, the different aches and pains, and knowing which is ok and which is alarming, the training can fail, or you can get injured.

Similar things can occur with data literacy learning (and many internal processes and programs in an organization). If the organization does not listen to the feedback that is coming through on a data literacy initiative, the organization can run into many problems that could be avoided. How can an organization ensure they are receiving the proper feedback?

First, establish clear and transparent communication. As I have worked with organizations, I find that a proper communication strategy and plan can help ensure the organization's data literacy plan hits fewer bumps and obstacles along the path. Plus, it can help the organization ensure the training is taken versus just another email in the background. Along with the clear communication, maintain a channel for direct communication, like a Slack or Microsoft Teams channel.

Another way to ensure a good, strong feedback loop is to conduct internal surveys with the data literacy initiative participants. These surveys should focus on the learning strategy that was deployed in the organization, how the courses are going, what gaps the learners may be experiencing, and more. When these surveys are partnered with the first step of clear and transparent communication, it can help the participants to be open and honest about what is and is not working. Finally, to ensure a good, strong feedback loop, conduct open-ended focus groups with the participants. These can be one-on-one or in groups. These groups should allow for discussions around the learning and plan. Like surveys, use these feedback groups to understand what is and is not working.

Overall, these feedback mechanisms can provide direct insight into a data literacy learning initiative an organization has taken on. Without these loops, organizations can experience large obstacles in the way of data literacy learning, which in turn can impact the overall data and analytical strategy. On the flipside, by having a strong feedback loop in your data literacy initiative, you can find the obstacles and gaps that are in the way of your success, improve them, and work towards a holistic strategy of success.

Step 5: Take the iterative approach to data literacy learning

Once we have the feedback mechanism in place, what do we do with the feedback? We run an iterative approach to our data literacy learning and program. What is an iterative approach, you may ask? Understanding what an iteration is can help.

Within the world of data and analytics, organizations are collecting more and more data. With the increase in data, organizations can update their models, get a clearer picture of a situation, and many other things. With that clearer picture and updated models, we can start to see improved decision-making and more. What would happen if the organization did not receive more data, more information, and only had the same model for years? Unfortunately, that would be a very dire and sad situation for whatever decisions were being made from that model; organizations would want new data to come into the system to help improve and iterate on the process.

This is the power of the feedback in step 4. The feedback coming into the data literacy initiative is like the new data coming into the model. It allows the leaders of the data literacy initiative to find those pieces that need to be changed and to iterate on the program. The word iteration means 'the action or a process of iterating or repeating: such as a procedure in which repetition of a sequence of operations yields results successively closer to a desired result'.[2] With a data literacy program, we are looking for strong learning within data and analytics in order for an organization to make better decisions with its data and give a strong return on investment. Iteration can play a key role in an organization truly finding the success it is looking for with investments in data.

Learning for the four characteristics of data literacy

It should come as no surprise that there is a section within this book on how to learn the four characteristics of data literacy. Let us make one thing clear: data literacy learning is a lifelong process. It isn't possible to put in one book, let alone a single chapter, all the things you could do to learn how to read, work with, analyze, and communicate with data. What we want to accomplish in this chapter, therefore, is to give you a few things you can do to learn the four characteristics better. We will begin with what may be the most important characteristic in the definition: reading data.

Characteristic 1: Read data

When we think of reading data, let's think of children learning to read a book. As a father myself, what is it that helps my child to learn how to read the most? In my family, I can look to a few key things: a mentor or teacher, exercises and deliberate practice (this will be a common method throughout all four characteristics), and, simply, just consistent reading practice (this is different from deliberate practice).

What do we mean by a mentor or teacher? With a parent to a child, it is one who knows how to read and is giving the lessons. For us, when we are learning to read data, we should find mentors and teachers, those who know or have the experience, and utilize them as our helpers. This doesn't necessarily mean an in-person way of learning. You can find the right mentor or teacher online. Ideally, this person should have a concrete ability to read data themselves and possess and ability to teach.

Next, as we are learning to read data, we should find different exercises and implement deliberate practice into our learning routine. Deliberate practice is a concept that has come more and more into vogue over the last decade or two. In essence, deliberate practice is not just routinely practicing the same thing over and over. It means finding key areas and skills to focus on and practicing those, improving those and then working harder until that skill becomes a part of who you are. You can use reading data exercises as part of deliberate practice, but don't just keep reading data over and over – find areas of weakness or areas where you lack skill and knowledge, then practice them.

Finally, you can just read, read, and then read some data some more. This is where you do the routine practicing. Find dashboards, data visualizations, books, and so forth that will help you learn to read data. Then, practice and read. When doing this, you will find that your skill in reading data becomes stronger and stronger.

Characteristic 2: Working with data

Like the others, we will see a theme in how we learn the four characteristics of data: find a mentor or teacher, find exercises and use deliberate practice, and, finally, practice, practice, practice.

When one is thinking of data, the key is what is your actual role in working with data? Are you a data analyst, a data scientist, do you have a leadership role or are you a decision-maker? Each of these roles is critical to the world of data and analytics, and data literacy is critical to these roles. To learn how to work with data, knowing your role with data matters.

When you are looking for a mentor, ensure you know what your role is and then find someone who has that skill. When you are finding exercises and using deliberate practice, ensure it is within your role. Exercises can be found through many, many channels: BI and analytics companies, such as Tableau or Qlik, YouTube, LinkedIn learning, and so forth. Find different avenues to learning how to work with data. Then, practice, practice, practice.

Characteristic 3: Analyzing data

Analyzing data is an interesting one when it comes to the four characteristics of data. When we think of the skill of analyzing data, it can come in different forms: are we talking analyzing data through statistics? Are we talking analyzing data through strong question making? Are we talking analyzing data through dashboards, data visualizations, and model building? Overall, like working with data, we want to ensure we understand what our role is. It won't make much sense for us to study statistics if it isn't something we will be using much. Now, we can study these things, but make sure we aren't biting off more than we can chew. Like with running, if we don't pace ourselves we will surely run out of steam before we've crossed the finish line.

In each case, it is like reading and working with data: find the right mentor or teacher, find the right exercises and deliberate practice, and then practice, practice, practice. With analyzing data, remember there are so many facets of this characteristic that the best place to start is to really assess your own skill level with these characteristics. Along with assessing your skill level, dig into the different areas and find the one you are passionate about, then jump in. This can be said about each and every characteristic: assess your skill level, study the different areas, and jump in.

Characteristic 4: Communicating with data

This last characteristic is a vital one to the process of good data and analysis, so learning good skills in this area is vital to properly implementing the insight and decision you have made. Communicating with data is so vital that McKinsey, the research firm, predicts that by 2026 the demand for an analytics translator (someone who can communicate with and about data) may reach 2 to 4 million in the United States alone.[3] This role is absolutely vital for data and analytical success in organizations. The role bridges the gap between data and analytics and the business. If you are learning one key skill within your data literacy repertoire, mastering the skill of communicating with data should be near or at the top of your list.

Like the other characteristics, a mentor or teacher is vital, exercises and deliberate practice are necessary, and overall practice should be complete. If you are looking to grow your ability, talk with others about data and analytics quite often, read and study words, then try them on others. Overall, communicating with data is a necessary skill to have. Remember, communicating with data also means the ability to understand and listen to data.

The four characteristics are a great way to assess your skills: how comfortable are you with each? Then, when you know your gaps, get to work.

Learning for a strong data literate culture

When it comes to data literacy and learning, there is one large hurdle organizations need to work to resolve, if it is not ready: the organization's culture. With the largest roadblock to data and analytical success being that of organizational culture, it stands to reason that an organization would need to address the culture. How can an organization ensure data literacy learning is strong and successful? What key characteristics should an organization adopt to help ensure the data literacy learning is successful, data and analytical strategy (including data and tool work) is adopted, and just overall data success? We will look at steps the organization can adopt and put in place to help the data literacy learning. Some of these will have been found throughout this book already, but look at them now from the holistic approach of what the organizational culture can do to succeed.

Adopt data democratization

When we democratize something, we give it to the masses. In this case, we are democratizing the data throughout the organization and putting it into the hands of the masses. This is a strong, powerful way to have data and analytical success at an organization. Giving it to the masses will allow the organization to get more eyes on the information, more creative minds looking into the data. With true, strong data democratization, ensure you partner it with the right data literacy learning. Doing these in tandem, the investment you make in both can be more successful.

Adopt transparency

What does transparency mean when it comes from the sense of data literacy? It means to be transparent, or open, with what you are doing with data. Give people the right access to democratization, allow access to the right data sets, and so forth. Now, transparency does not mean a free-for-all, and neither does true democratization of data, but it means giving the right access, at the right access point, and having a strong, open communication plan for the workforce. Do not keep quiet on what you are doing with data; let it be known, and let people voice their thoughts and opinions on the manner.

Adopt learning

This should be no surprise in a chapter on learning data literacy, but an organization needs to adopt a learning strategy, and this chapter should help with things to do.

Adopt mentoring

Mentoring can be a key to success within data and analytics. When we think of mentoring, we think of the traditional one-on-one mentoring programs that organizations put in place. Adopt this type of program for mentoring within data and analytics. Are you good at creating viable and impactful data visualizations? That is fantastic, mentor on it. Are you good at asking strong questions of the data, allowing the organization to find answers? That is an unbelievable skill, share it and help others learn how to ask those questions.

One thing to understand, though, when it comes to a culture of data literacy learning, mentoring does not only mean mentoring on a one-on-one basis; expand it to the wider company. Explore options such as holding a 30-minute lunch-and-learn, where people can bring their lunches to sit back and learn at your feet. In a virtual environment, invite people to grab their favorite snack, sit back, and have you teach them. The key is to create a culture of mentoring and teaching others, so the skills start to flow throughout the organization. One thing this will lend itself to: data fluency.

Adopting data fluency

This topic has been spoken of in detail, so it will only be mentioned briefly here in the backdrop of a data-driven and data literacy culture. If an organization's culture wants data and analytics to succeed, and its data literacy strategy to thrive, data fluency can be the perfect ingredient to make the recipe of data and analytics successful. When the organization's culture as a whole speaks the language of data, the same language of data, then the organization can thrive.

Picture a data point, analysis, or insight. When an organization has an insight flowing through it, those working on the data points and insight can share it with the different groups throughout the organization. Then, no matter what the organization skill set, the comfort with data fluency, and speaking that language, the insight can be implemented in decisions, and people are comfortable with what has happened.

Adopt leadership support

Have you ever tried to do something at your company or in your career where you do not have your leadership's support? How did that go for you? You want to have leadership buy-in for a culture program on data literacy. That said, when doing your own independent learning, that is ok. If you want to drive an organization program, then get that buy-in for sure.

Culture summary

Overall, culture is the number one roadblock to your success within data and analytics. Data literacy, empowering individuals with better learning and skills, will naturally help your culture to thrive better with data and analytics. To take your culture to the next level, adopt the characteristics above.

Other areas of data literacy learning and focus

There are a few things that are a part of the data literacy umbrella that need proper learning in the organization, which we will cover as we conclude the chapter.

Data ethics

Data ethics is such an important topic: how do we use data correctly? There must be learning around this topic. Organizations need to empower their workforce to understand how to use data correctly. The reality is, the later 2010s saw the ethical use of data come to the forefront. Laws and regulations were passed to help with data ethics. As time moves on, more regulations, thoughts, ideas, and possibly laws may be passed on artificial intelligence and machine learning. To help the organization succeed with data and analytics, ensure people have a strong understanding and learning of data ethics.

Data science

This may seem a weird one to put in here because not everyone needs to be a data scientist – we just want to expand on data literacy. The key here is to create learning opportunities within two different channels: 1) learning what data science truly is (I mean, it is a mysterious world) and 2) helping the data scientists and organization work together. We want the organization to understand what data science is and, maybe more importantly, what it is not. By helping the organization learn this, the organization can have realistic expectations of the data scientists in their work (no, the data scientist is not going to create a model and analysis for you that will solve all your ills and work troubles). Second, we want the data scientists to learn more about the business, their role in it, and so forth. By allowing that learning to take place within data science, power can be created for data and analytical success.

Data quality

Ensure you build into your data literacy strategy learning on data quality. If the individuals who are using and working with data do not understand the purpose and need for data quality, we are not sitting in a strong position for great and powerful insight. What good will the insight be, if the data has no quality within the model? Teach the back-end architects the absolute need to ensure quality for the front-end users and teach the front-end users the absolute need to communicate effectively with the architects on your needs (see, the power of data fluency happens again).

These are just a few of the other areas where an organization needs to ensure there is an education scheme and a strategy. Far too often, individuals and organizations will focus on the 'big-ticket items' and ensure there is learning in these areas, but they skip some of the other 'unknown' areas. To work towards ensuring you don't miss these areas, do regular check-ins with yourself and within the organization you work with. If you have gaps, find the gaps, assess what is missing, build a learning plan, be transparent, and then execute.

Chapter summary

With the topic of data literacy, it is not a coincidence that the world of learning is essential. Since not everyone is going to school to develop backgrounds within the field of data and analytics, even with the hopes and push for more STEM or STEAM education, we need to ensure organizations are implementing a sound, strong learning strategy for everyone to succeed. If you are an individual, set your goals and desires and implement your own plan.

In this chapter, we covered key areas of learning within the vast world of data literacy. Each one of these key areas of learning matters to your organization. Look to the role of leadership to drive your learning strategy. Ensure the data and analytical strategy your organization has implemented includes data literacy learning. Follow a strong learning framework and approach. Ensure your data literacy learning strategy has some focus on the four characteristics of the definition of data literacy: reading, working with, analyzing, and communicating with data. Work to have your culture succeed with data literacy, and finally, look at where the gaps are in your learning and hit them hard with a strong plan.

Data literacy learning can be fun, insightful, and empowering, for both an individual and an organization. Find where you need the help and hit the ground running. The world we live in needs a much more data literate society, not just for our careers, but also for life in general.

Notes

1 Qlik (undated) Data-Informed Decision-making Framework. Available from: https://learning.qlik.com/course/view.php?id=1021 (archived at https://perma.cc/4VPF-FQQG)

2 Merriam-Webster Dictionary (undated) Definition of Iteration. Available from: https://www.merriam-webster.com/dictionary/iteration (archived at https://perma.cc/M3YT-ZJ7P)

3 Henke, N, Levin, J, McInerney, P (2018) Analytics Translator: The New Must-Have Role, McKinsey, 1 February. Available from: https://www.mckinsey.com/business-functions/mckinsey-analytics/our-insights/analytics-translator# (archived at https://perma.cc/K5V7-L9V2)

08

The three Cs of data literacy

In Chapter 7, we took a look at the ways an organization can implement and put in place strong data literacy learning… but, this is from the organizational level. An organization is made up of individuals, and not just individuals, but individuals with different personalities and skill sets. One of the top questions I get from people is: 'How do I start my data literacy journey?' If we are looking to build out an organizational strategy and truly want it to succeed, we need to also focus on the individuals. This leads to a new set of questions: what should individuals study and do they need to study statistics?

The quick answer is no, you don't have to be a data scientist or statistician, we know this. We do have to put the right learning in place so that each individual that participates in their own data literacy journey has an effective engagement. There are a few things an individual can do before going into the specific world of data literacy learning, which we have explored: the three Cs of data literacy.

The three Cs of data literacy are: curiosity, creativity, and critical thinking. To help us understand the three Cs of data literacy, we are going to explore them within the vein of two pillars: the pillar of data literacy characteristics (reading, working with, analyzing, and arguing with data) and the pillar of analytics (the four levels of analytics). By diving into these areas, we will give the reader the opportunity to see how 1) this is implemented in data and analytical work and 2) how they personally may be able to implement this in their careers and lives. One thing for everyone who is looking to advance data literacy in their careers is that data literacy can also be implemented in their personal lives. The three Cs should become an everyday part of our lives.

The first C of data literacy: Curiosity

The first C of data literacy is curiosity. I am fond of saying, 'They say curiosity killed the cat, but I say curiosity spurred on data literacy.' When we think of curiosity, what does it bring to our minds? For me, a father, I think of children. One thing that is endearing about children is their rampant curiosity. Children are always asking questions, about everything. Why is that? They are trying to figure things out. There is a problem with us as we leave childhood: we lose our curiosity! We sit and get data and information presented to us on a consistent basis as adults, but how often are we curious about it? Unfortunately, we usually aren't asking many questions. We usually see it, take it, and move forward. We need to bring out curiosity out more and more; we need to ask more questions. Questions can open so many doors within the world of data and analytics. In fact, the definition of the word curiosity is: 'the urge you feel to know more about something'.[1] That definition shows us a lot about the word curiosity. Let's start the process by looking at curiosity within the definition of data literacy.

Within the first characteristic of data literacy, the ability to read data and curiosity might as well be brother and sister. As we read data and information, which means the ability to look at the data and information and comprehend what is there, it should spark our curiosity. Then, this curiosity and reading data can help to spark questions within us to learn more about the data and information that is presented to us. This allows us to read more and more, and the cycle continues.

A good example of reading data to learn more is when an executive leader is confident in their data literacy ability. When an individual presents to them a result or KPI dashboard, the executive can read the data, then their curiosity will grow and they will ask the person to produce more and more data. This should be done not only at the executive level, but at all levels of the organization.

With reading data, we can see a natural transition into the world of curiosity and working with data. When an individual is reading the information and understands it, they can then work with the data to find more information and results. Then, as they read the information, they can work with the data more and the cycle continues. A good example of working with data and curiosity comes to us from the world of data visualization building. When an individual builds a powerful and insights driven data and analytics dashboard, depending on the software used (like Qlik or Tableau), the individual will be able to use different filtering, drop downs, and tabs to work further with the data. With curiosity, we might take a look at a dashboard and wonder what more it may contain. For example, take a look at the dashboard in Figure 8.1.

This dashboard shows my training for a certain race: the Leadville 100 ultra-marathon. With curiosity, we may ask ourselves why are some of the distance bars bigger than others? What does the darker color mean for the different trainers? Is it that I like the trainer or more, or was the workout that much more effective? The myriad list of questions can go on and on. With this curiosity, we can break down the overall visualization, filter it, and get answers to our questions, or at least start to get answers and, if we are curious, create a list of other questions

This dovetails right into the third characteristic of data literacy, that is analyzing the data. Let's take a look at another data visualization in Figure 8.2 – what has been happening with real estate prices and commissions?

As a real estate agent, you are trying to determine the trend of home prices, commissions, and so forth. In this case, we can ask questions, such as what drove the average price up on the days where the darker orange/red is evident? We also can take a look at the average commission and rate each day. We can ask whether this is staying the same or varying. With all of this information, we can analyze the data with our curiosity. Our curiosity should spark within us a keen desire to analyze the information and be ready to ask more questions, get more answers, and come to the right decision.

FIGURE 8.1 Leadville training plan

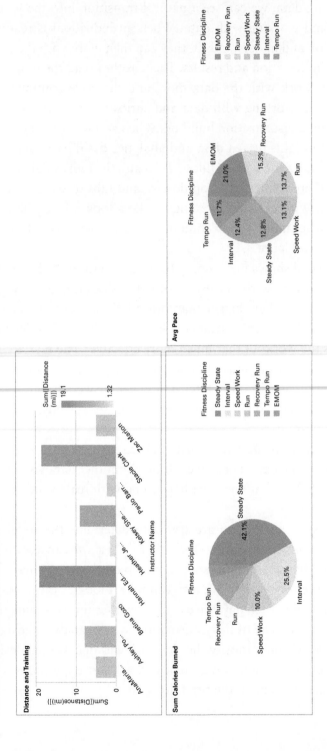

FIGURE 8.2   Real estate study example

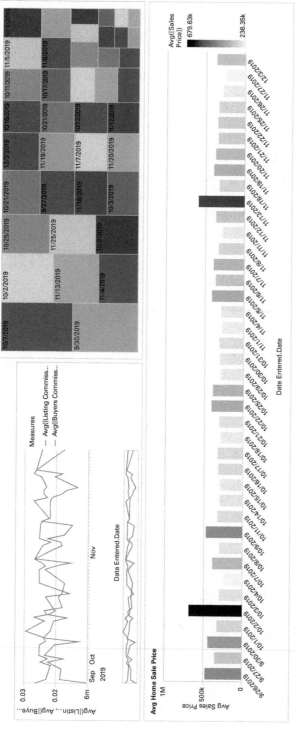

The final characteristic is of course communication with data. Communication is an essential piece of the puzzle. As we are looking to communicate with data effectively, it is crucial we have the ability to use curiosity to do this. You may ask yourself: how does curiosity help? Well, in our case, it can help us to ask questions such as: will this audience receive this information effectively if I communicate it like this? What is the audience I am presenting to? How long should I communicate this? What kind of statistics should I use? The list can go on.

Overall, all four characteristics in the definition of data literacy matter with the first C of data literacy: curiosity. Also, we should now be able to see how the four levels of analytics also matter with the world of curiosity.

FIGURE 8.3   John Snow's cholera visualization, 1854

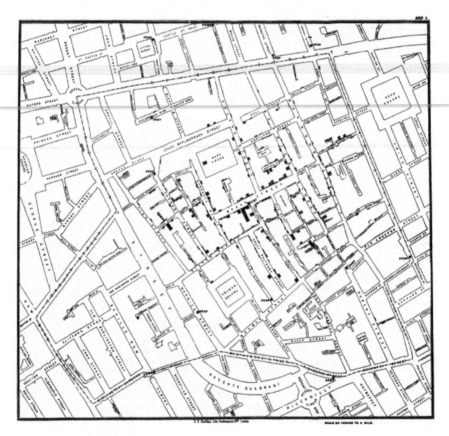

Now, to transition to the four levels of analytics shouldn't be too hard. The four levels of analytics, if you remember, are descriptive, diagnostic, predictive, and prescriptive. The curiosity of an individual should help to shape, shift, and expound the four levels of analytics. To help us understand this, let's turn back to the famous cholera visualization we looked at in a previous chapter (Figure 8.3).

Curiosity is such a great tool to utilize for data literacy within the four levels of analytics and this cholera visualization. Remember, this visualization helped open the door to both data journalism and to help subside and improve the cholera outbreak. How can curiosity help?

First, descriptive analytics. Now, a hypothetical scenario: imagine if John Snow utilized curiosity to visualize the outbreak itself. In this case, visualizing the data was a curious idea. I can picture John Snow saying to himself: 'Where are all these outbreaks happening? Do we have any data that shows where the outbreaks occurred?' Through these questions, he was able to build out this beautiful data visualization. What other descriptive analytics questions could John Snow have asked? He could have asked, 'Are there certain demographics that are being impacted by the outbreak more than others?' or 'Are there other areas of town experiencing this type of outbreak?' These are great questions that help further the first level of analytics for John Snow to help resolve and provide solutions for the cholera outbreak.

One key thing to note within the sphere of the four levels of analytics, and in particular descriptive analytics, is the power of a data visualization that both 1) came from curiosity and 2) sparked more curiosity to help resolve the outbreak. This book focuses not on data visualizations themselves – you can find many of those to read – but on data literacy. In this case, though, and in many others, the data visualization was an amazing starting point to powerful and impactful data-driven decision-making. We cannot underestimate this powerful tool and important piece of data and analytics.

The second level of analytics is diagnostic. Here, I can picture John Snow asking some very powerful and curious questions. Here are some questions that could have come from John Snow himself: 'Why is the brewery not experiencing so many outbreaks?' This is such a great question, because the cholera infection was coming from water.

Through diagnostic analytics, it could be determined that the workers at the brewery were not drinking water but beer. This difference can come from the curious diagnostic analytics question of John Snow. Another question I can see John Snow asking is: 'Why do we see clustered outbreaks in certain areas?' This very curious diagnostic question is such a powerful way to really start to home in on the data visualization.

Herein we see why data visualization is not the only answer to data and analytics, the treasure at the end of the rainbow, but it is the starting point. The visualization did not give us the 'why' behind the questions John Snow may have asked, but it did give us a starting point and that is absolutely critical. This touches upon another point: the 'why' behind the descriptive analytics. In John Snow's case, we have the ability to ask why many times to analyze the data. Then, when analyzing the data, we dig deep into the data, information, etc., to find better answers. For John Snow, his final 'why' question could have been: 'Why do we see such a cluster around the waterspout (the pump)?' It could have been questions just like this that led to the discovering of the dirty diaper/s that were found to pollute the water coming out of the common waterspout. This leads us to the third level of analytics, predictive analytics.

Predictive analytics is a great way to dissect both the diagnostic and descriptive levels of analytics. Herein we can supplant ourselves back to the cholera outbreak and John Snow's time and ask ourselves to make some predictions. Through the descriptive analytic that John built for us, we can then start to make observations that lead to questions of 'why' with regards to the data. Now that we have the 'why' questions and are looking into possible resolutions and answers, we have the ability to build out our modeling to help alleviate the area of cholera: Prediction = What if I remove the diaper/s from the water source or from infiltrating the water, what will that do? Well, in this case, it can help do a lot. Using our curiosity, we are able to make other predictions that could have been implemented in the area during the cholera outbreak.

For example, one prediction we could make is that it isn't the diaper/s themselves, but the waterspout. So, let's replace the waterspout and see what this will accomplish for the community. Well, in this case, it wouldn't have done much, but this is a part of iterative analytics. We try to implement something, get results, and then keep going. I bet we wouldn't have been hired if we said forget the dirty, contaminated water from diaper/s, let's just replace the pump. Personally, I am not hiring that firm.

Another prediction we could have made with our curiosity: those working at the brewery and drinking alcohol are not experiencing cholera the same. Our prediction is if we take everyone off water and onto the local favorite drink, we will see a subsiding of the outbreak. The reality is they probably would have seen that happen and people maybe would have liked this solution more, but we really didn't get to the root cause of the issue. We found what is called spurious correlation, where two things seem related but they are not. In other words, correlation did not equate to causation, which is a standard fallacy among data analysis and should be a part of everyone's data literacy handbook. In any case, and in our case specifically, the suggestion or prediction that beer would help if we drank it instead of water is true, but doesn't truly solve any problem. In fact, maybe it would cause more. What if the demand for alcohol became so strong the brewery would have to start using water from that pump? We may be right back at square one.

The final level of analytics is prescriptive analytics. Prescriptive analytics, again, is essentially letting the data and technology tell you how to do things. In this case, our curiosity should be in place to ask questions of what the technology is telling us and what the predictions and prescriptive analytics are showing us. Not to mention the desire to challenge the assumptions the modeling makes.

The final area of curiosity we want to explore has been mentioned here and this needs direct attention: correlation versus causation. When we are curious and asking question after question, it becomes imperative we do not become stuck in a curiosity trap where we think that correlation means causation. We are going to be visiting analytics and interesting relationships in data throughout our careers and lives. Sometimes, when we are curious and looking at the data and information, we may see something that looks like one thing is causing another.

There are many examples of this in the world, but let me give a quick example with regards to data and the business world. Spurious correlation – the perceived existence of a relationship between two things, where one is thought to drive another – is a key term to learn.

Imagine to yourself that you are the marketing director for a large soda company, maybe Pepsi or Coca-Cola. You are launching an amazing ad campaign in April this year, hoping to really hit a gold mine. You launch the campaign and start your curiosity journey: Did my latest marketing campaign help drive an increase in revenue and sales? First, to start off, this is a fine question to ask, but we must be careful. With your curiosity, you have built a data visualization to look at the results. By looking at the results, you see that the trend line for revenue is going up, starting in May and going through August. Since you launched the campaign at the end of April, your curiosity to look at the data and see success was rewarded – eureka! You have stuck gold! There is a problem here though: we have assumed the marketing campaign was the cause of the revenue increase. We have made an assumption, but let our curiosity stop because maybe, just maybe, our personal bias kicked in and we saw what we wanted to see. What if it wasn't the marketing campaign at all, but that those were summer months in two large markets: Europe and the USA? Maybe it was just the summer months kicking in and people were hot, turning to their favorite sodas for refreshment. We need to ensure we do not stop our curiosity but drive it through the different levels of analytics. Doing this can ensure we don't stop too soon, rely on faulty and incorrect information, and then let that lead to poor predictions.

The second C of data literacy: Creativity

The second C of data literacy is one of my favorite pieces within the world of data and analytics: creativity. It is my feeling that the most powerful computer in the world is the human mind. No, I do not mean by computing speed or power, but the overall ability of the human mind to bring creativity and power to the things we take on and look to accomplish. One of the most beautiful aspects of the human mind is that no two minds are exactly alike. The way I think is different from the way you think, which is different from every other reader of this book. It is this power that allows us to really bring the creativity of the human element to data and analytics. The human element is the essence of data literacy. One of my favorite quotes is said to come from Albert Einstein, though this is not proven, but it reads: 'Everybody is a genius. But if you judge a fish by its ability to climb a tree, it will live its whole life believing that it is stupid.'[2]

Whether or not this quote comes from Albert Einstein, and I hope it does, is irrelevant to the conversation. What matters is the premise: not everyone is the same and everyone has genius built into them. If we try to build everyone up the exact same way, we are going to fail in our adventure. In the world of data literacy, we have to understand that data literacy is not a one-stop shop for each individual. We cannot teach everyone the exact same way. If we do, we are eliminating genius by telling everyone they need to be a fish, regardless of the tree. Within data and analytics, we need to unleash the creative genius that exists within each individual, while incorporating the corporate methodology to deploying enterprise-wide data literacy initiatives. If we unleash this creativity correctly, we are not only going to unleash the power of each individual's curiosity, but also their creative skills to great and successful means. The first thing we must do is understand how creativity plays a part in each characteristic of the definition of data literacy.

What does creativity even mean? In order to tie it to the four characteristics of data literacy, we must understand its powerful definition. 'The ability to transcend traditional ideas, rules, patterns, relationships, or the like, and to create meaningful new ideas, forms, methods, interpretations, etc.; originality, progressiveness, or imagination' is the definition from Dictionary.com.[3] I don't think we need to write more after that definition. This touches upon every aspect and part of data literacy where creativity needs to be a part of the equation. I especially love multiple parts of this definition. First, the ability to transcend traditional ideas. When we think of data and analytics, many think it is boring. Now, we can see there is a new breakthrough with our own personal creativity being added to the story. We are breaking down the traditional norms and hitting it home with new ideas and thoughts. Second, look at the position of creating 'meaningful new ideas' and

FIGURE 8.4 My wife and my mother-in-law

SOURCE *Puck*, v. 78, no. 2018 (1915 6 Nov.), p. 11

how it impacts data and analysis. By taking a new perspective, we are absolutely finding new ways to analyze the data.

As we have done, let us look at the second C of data literacy in light of the four characteristics found within the definition of data literacy, and we will combine in the definition of creativity. The first characteristic is reading data, where creativity absolutely can be brought to the forefront. Let us examine the famous image in Figure 8.4

What do you see here in this picture? Is it an older woman with a little bit of a smile, or is it the side of a face of a young woman? This is the brilliance of this image, as it can be either, or if you are like me you can switch between the two images. This is the power of creativity when looking at data.

While it is true that the number 1,204,513 is going to be 1,204,513, what if we are looking at the representation of data through an image or visualization? That is the power of each and every one of us: we have the power to use our personal creativity to see the story differently. The saying is that an image speaks a thousand words, and in our case, a data visualization can speak to us in many different ways. Whether we see the old woman or the different clustering of cholera, we have the ability to get creative with the data. Do not get slowed down by a lack of creativity or where an analysis is hit with paralysis. Utilize your creativity to read the data in your own way. Who knows, maybe your way holds the key to open the golden nugget of truth within the data.

The same can be said for the second characteristic of the definition of data literacy: working with data. We can all build a table in Excel, but how creative is that? What if we utilize the power of Tableau or Qlik to build a brilliant visualization while working with data? Not only this, but what if we take a beautiful data visualization, use our creativity, and say: 'I wonder if the data within this chart would show us anything different if we built this kind of data visualization?' The ability of our minds to be creative is endless, as we are all unique. When working with data, we should not be settling to just continue the same old charts of yesterday. A personal example from my career can help shed some light on this working with data.

In a prior position, I ran analytics on a certain type of loan reserve for portfolios. When I entered into this job, I inherited a mess of a PowerPoint report. This report was about 75–80 slides long, with each slide mainly being made up of one chart. You read that right: one chart per slide in this report and it was 75–80 slides long. The best part? Each chart was built in Excel, so I would have to update the file each week and ensure the charts worked properly and the links were in place. If I accidently broke a link in the data, then the PowerPoint slides would not update and I would have to link each chart in its slide again. This was not a fun process, especially since this report went to executives and leadership, so making sure it was clean and accurate was important in and of itself.

As I owned and updated this report, I thought of a creative, new way to build it. Instead of having it all be charts within Excel, and a mountain of charts at that, I built six predictive chart models. That is right: just six! Not only was it just six charts at this point, but the intended audience was able to view them on their phones. Goodbye PowerPoint nightmare from the underworld and hello efficiency. This came about from my creativity.

The third characteristic in the definition of data literacy is that of analyzing data. What do you think creativity has to do with analyzing data? Plenty! When we analyze data, one of the key aspects of analyzing data is the ability to ask good questions. If we all were to ask the same questions, can you imagine how poor our data analysis would be? As we expand our data literacy skill set and develop top-of-the-line skills within data and analytics, our ability to bring in our personal perspective and creativity becomes more and more powerful. One strong aspect of this world of bringing our own creativity to analyzing data comes from STEM education.

STEM education focuses on science, technology, engineering, and mathematics. I have been a loud and vocal advocate of adding one more letter to STEM education and I have been happy to see its evolution in late 2019 and early 2020: *STEAM* education. It now can be read: science, technology, engineering, arts, and mathematics. The advent of the arts in data and analytics is not new but thankfully it is getting a bigger and wider audience. The arts enable us to not only read, work with, and analyze data, but also tap into the fourth characteristic as well: communicating with data.

Communicating with data is such a needed and powerful aspect of data and analytics. When we look at the world of data and analytics, it is no secret that, at times, it is boring, intimidating, and fear-inducing. Not everyone is a nerd such as myself and loves this world, so the ability to communicate data and analyses effectively matters very, very much. I can step into the world of the second C of data literacy: creativity. Within creativity, and the arts, is the power to tie a story together, create context, and bring power to the audience. As we develop our data literacy skills and really develop the ability to tell a good story with data, creativity becomes an essential part. With this creativity, many others can partake in and understand key aspects and solutions to data. Imagine how much more powerful your entire career in data and analytics could have been had better context, understanding, and intention been brought to the table. This can be done through the power of creativity.

Now that we have built out and understood the power of data and analysis, we need to tie in creativity to the four levels of analytics. Each level can be tied in directly with the world of creativity, as creativity allows both the practitioner and organization to find how the world of data and analytics can wind together.

The first level of analytics is, of course, descriptive analytics. Within descriptive analytics, it can be very easy to build a data visualization. Reporting on KPIs and the data can be very straightforward. This is actually one possible reason why organizations are stuck in the first level of analytics: it is quick and easy to build a descriptive analytic, without creativity. As many are good at reading data that just describes what happened in the prior month or quarter, this may not be sparking the interest in people to dig into the 'why' behind the descriptive analytic. If this is the case, creativity can help drive a descriptive analytic to do more. With descriptive analytics, such as data visualizations, built to drive more insight and to help people get to the 'why', creativity is the enabling power.

With this enabling creativity in the first level of analytics, it empowers the organization to jump into the second level of analytics: diagnostic analytics. With more creativity within the world of descriptive analytics, diagnostic analytics can really take flight. As you hone your skills to ask better questions of the data and information in front of you, you can then take different maps and routes to understanding the 'why' behind everything happening in the organization, your life, or any other aspect of data analysis that is taking place. Use your creative skills to find new insight, new answers, and new things that will drive insight to the world. Insight truly is the magic potion that comes from diagnostic analytics. With creativity, you are giving extra muscle to that magic potion.

Within the last two levels of analytics, creativity can play a great role in how 1) the predictive analytics are built, and 2) the predictive analytics are interpreted. Within these two levels, as models and analyses are built, it can be a very creative thing for the analysts and data scientists to look at how the model is built and deployed, helping us to ensure we are not just using the same model repeatedly. If all we do is the same thing over and over again, we may as well expect the same results over and over again. But, when we deploy a creative model, one we haven't tried before, and so forth, we may find new predictions and results. This also plays a part in how we interpret the models and analyses. If we use the same techniques to understand and analyze the models, we are not exercising creativity as much as we should. We need to use our personal abilities and skills within creativity to read the results in new ways, take a look at it from a new angle, and derive better insight.

To conclude on creativity, let's jump back into the definition from Dictionary.com: 'The ability to transcend traditional ideas, rules, patterns, relationships, or the like, and to create meaningful new ideas, forms, methods, interpretations, etc.; originality, progressiveness, or imagination.'[4] In rereading this definition, it should become very apparent why creativity is needed in the world of data literacy, data, and analytics: we need a new perspective, new thought process, and new understanding brought to the world of data and analytics. For far too long, the same old things have been done with data and analytics, whether it is using Excel, building the same types of data visualizations, or turning to your favorite statistical model over and over again. Stop it now! Start to dig into the world of getting creative with your data and analytical work. You won't regret bringing in a little more creativity to your work.

The third C of data literacy: Critical thinking

The third C of data literacy may be one of the most powerful within the world of data and analytics: critical thinking. Within the world of data and analytics, and in our lives in general, there may not be a more important time than the current data and digital revolution to implement stronger skills and backgrounds within critical thinking. From understanding elections and what politicians put in front of us (whether it is accurate or a bunch of, well, something that is not so pleasant), to understanding the world of pandemics and the data presented, to decision-making within our own lives, critical thinking is absolutely necessary. The definition of critical thinking from Dictionary.com is 'disciplined thinking that is clear, rational, open-minded, and informed by evidence'.[5] That seems pretty straightforward, but it does not occur within the world of data and analysis enough.

There is a great quote by the astrophysicist Carl Sagan from his book *The Demon Haunted World*:

> I have a foreboding of an America in my children's or grandchildren's time – when the United States is a service and information economy; when nearly all the manufacturing industries have slipped away to other countries; when awesome technological powers are in the hands of a very few, and no one representing the public interest can even grasp the issues; when the people have lost the ability to set their own agendas or knowledgeably question those in authority; when, clutching our crystals and nervously consulting our horoscopes, our critical faculties in decline, unable to distinguish between what feels good and what's true, we slide, almost without noticing, back into superstition and darkness...
>
> The dumbing down of American is most evident in the slow decay of substantive content in the enormously influential media, the 30 second sound bites (now down to 10 seconds or less), lowest common denominator programming, credulous presentations on pseudoscience and superstition, but especially a kind of celebration of ignorance.[6]

This quote was published in 1995. I would say we are definitely in this age envisioned by Carl Sagan. I believe one key area that hinders us in this day and age of technology, fast-updating social media and more is a lack of critical thinking. This lack of critical thinking absolutely crushes an individual's ability to succeed with data literacy. The four characteristics of data literacy will show us this.

Reading data

The first characteristic, as we know, is reading data. We have a great ability as we are reading data to critically think about what we are reading. Whether it is the latest sports update, a news update, the latest company memo or dashboard, and so forth. Critically thinking, as it says in the definition, is the ability to think on the material in a disciplined fashion, being open-minded, and informed by evidence. When new data and information is presented to us, do we look at it with a disciplined front? When we see news during the COVID-19 pandemic, do we jump to conclusions, or do we rationally and openly think about it? This type of thinking is very important within the world of politics. Politicians, and companies advertising for that matter, are trying to sway us left and right. Do we think about it with an open mind? Are we straightforward in what we are reading? Critical thinking while we are reading data can really set the stage for good, strong analysis. If we do not critically think on what we are reading, we are setting the foundation of our analytical home on sandy foundations.

Working with data

As we read the data, working with data with a critical thinking eye can be crucial for good analysis. As we build a data visualization, work in a statistical model, review a dashboard or KPIs, we are able to look at the data and information with a critical eye to sound, solid data analysis. As we discussed with critical thinking and reading data, we need to ensure we are doing the same with working with data. While we work with data, we are able to ensure the decisions we will make with the data come out the way we want them to. Like we discussed with building the foundation of an analysis correctly by critically thinking while reading data, we now can build the walls of our home on our foundation through critically thinking while working with data.

Analyzing data

The third characteristic of analyzing data and the third C of data literacy, critical thinking, work together in a manner much like reading data. As we analyze data, we have the ability to just look for answers we want to see versus the answers we should see within the data. Critical thinking allows us to work through analyzing data in a manner in which we can find objective truth or information in the data. This really ties to the end of the definition of critical thinking: informed by evidence. We need to ensure as we analyze the data and information presented to us that we critically think on it. No more only looking at the data and information we like, no more looking only for our answers, but truly being open to our minds being changed, to our preconceived notions being altered, and an overall shift in mindset. Analyzing data can not only be powerful for insight and information, but it can be mind- and life-altering for us personally. Within our house-building analogy, we are now building out the walls with analyzing data.

Communicating with data

The final characteristic of data literacy has a unique aspect and place in the world of critical thinking. As we build out communications with data and analytics, we need to think about two things to ensure we are in a strong critical thinking position: the best way to share this information, and identifying the audience. By critically thinking on these positions, we are in a spot to really ensure our communications are done and received effectively. Within our growing house analogy, the roof can now be put on with critical thinking and communicating with data.

The four levels of analytics are similar to the four characteristics of the definition of data literacy. The first level of descriptive analytics can be viewed in two different ways with critical thinking: one with developing the data visualization or report, and two with the interpretation therein. While we are developing a data visualization or building a dashboard/report, we have the ability to critically think on what we have built and are building. As we build it out, we can ask questions around our descriptive analytic: Is this being built properly? Am I capturing enough information to make it valuable? Is there another way I can present this and give more value to the audience? Then, as we interpret the information in descriptive analytics, we can ask similar questions to ensure our interpretation is strong, effective, and powerful.

The second level of analytics, diagnostic analytics, is a lot like the analyze characteristic of data literacy: analyzing data. As we are looking to find the 'why' behind the data and information we have in front of us with descriptive analytics, we must follow the definition from Dictionary.com: 'disciplined thinking that is clear, rational, open-minded, and informed by evidence'.[7] As we build out the why, we need to ensure we are clear, rational, open-minded (maybe most especially here), and informed by evidence. By being open-minded we can hopefully not be steered away by our own bias, the bias of others, incorrect ideas, and more. This allows us to truly find the 'why' behind the data and analysis.

The third and fourth levels of analytics are also powerful from a critical-thinking perspective, and like the data visualization building and interpretation, when we are dealing with the third and fourth levels of analytics, we are looking at critical thinking at both the building/modeling level and the interpretation level. As maybe a practitioner who is building the analyses and models, one needs to critically think into the model and analysis, ensuring it is open-minded and informed by evidence. As we interpret these levels of analytics, we need to keep our minds open and as we keep being informed by evidence, both internal and external, we can ensure we are critically thinking through all the levels.

Chapter summary

The three Cs of data literacy – curiosity, creativity, and critical thinking – are essential to strong data literacy work. As we work hard to implement these as individuals, both in our careers and in our lives, we can work towards smarter, sounder decision-making. In addition, we can work towards and succeed with our overall data and analytical work. Remember, as you work through the four characteristics of the definition of data literacy and as we work through the four levels of analytics, the three Cs play a great and critical role within each.

Notes

1 Vocabulary.com (undated) Definition of Curiosity. Available from: https://www. vocabulary.com/dictionary/curiosity (archived at https://perma.cc/3ZVH-VFF8)
2 Quote Investigator (undated) Available from: https://quoteinvestigator. com/2013/04/06/fish-climb/ (archived at https://perma.cc/W7ZQ-P7JM)
3 Dictionary.com (undated) Definition of Creativity. Available from: https://www. dictionary.com/browse/creativity (archived at https://perma.cc/H3D4-JCVX)
4 Dictionary.com (undated) Definition of Creativity. Available from: https://www. dictionary.com/browse/creativity (archived at https://perma.cc/H3D4-JCVX)
5 Dictionary.com (undated) Definition of Critical Thinking. Available from: https://www.dictionary.com/browse/critical-thinking?s=t (archived at https:// perma.cc/V45R-6BLZ)
6 Goodreads.com (undated) Carl Sagan Quote. Available from: https://www. goodreads.com/quotes/632474-i-have-a-foreboding-of-an-america-in-my- children-s (archived at https://perma.cc/4DKQ-PFS7)
7 Dictionary.com (undated) Definition of Critical Thinking. Available from: https://www.dictionary.com/browse/critical-thinking?s=t (archived at https:// perma.cc/V45R-6BLZ)

09

Data informed decision-making

We have spent the first eight chapters of this book discussing the why, what, and how of data literacy. Now, a big question: To what end? Why have I spent this time explaining data literacy? Was it so we would know how to build out pretty charts and data visualization? The answer is an emphatic '*No!*' Data literacy will not amount to anything if we do not know the end we are moving toward. That end is a decision. Data literacy should lead to an insight that then leads to a decision. If all we are doing with data literacy is coming up with the insight, then we do nothing with it. This is like finding a treasure map and not using it to find the buried treasure, or being given the lottery numbers before they are pulled but not buying a ticket. The end goal of data literacy should be to lead an individual or organization to make smart, data informed decision-making. How to do this will be the focus of this chapter.

Within the world and the framework of data and analytics, the art of decision-making can be overlooked quite easily. As organizations and individuals invest in the quality, sourcing, and tools that make up the world of data and analytics, decision-making should be at or near the top of the list of empowerments. For each individual and organization to succeed within this aspect of data literacy, a strong framework should be utilized. To help us establish a solid footing and foundation for each of us, we are going to turn to a strong framework put out by my friend and colleague, Kevin Hanegan and Qlik.[1] In this brilliant framework, we will walk through the six different steps that are needed to powerfully make smart, data informed decisions.

Please note for this book's purpose we are utilizing the term 'data informed' versus 'data driven'. This is on purpose, but I do concede that in most cases data driven is used in the world today. The term 'data driven' really gained steam in the late 2010s and into 2020, and especially moved forward with the onslaught of the worldwide COVID-19 pandemic. To be data driven means many things to many people, but ultimately it means data is strongly being used as an asset for an individual or organization. Think of it as a marathon runner using a plan to drive a strategy for a successful marathon. This is what data driven or data informed means. It means that data is helping to drive decisions and the business forward. The reason I use the term data informed over data driven is that with the term data driven one can make the mistake in thinking that the data is truly driving everything. Data informed means the data was used to help make the decision, but is combined with other things, like the human element. This distinction matters as it is powerful.

To help us understand data informed decisions and their combination with data literacy, we will be digging into our entire bag of tricks of data literacy. We will start by defining the framework and its power to drive decision-making. We will be looking at the data informed decision-making framework from what may seem like all possible angles: the four characteristics of the definition of data literacy, the four levels of analytics, speaking the language of data, the three Cs of data literacy, and probably more angles. For us to get started here, we need to know the steps of the data informed decision-making framework.

Steps of the data informed decision-making framework

The data informed decision-making framework we are employing for this book has six steps. Please note, there are different frameworks that exist in the world for making a decision, but for a strong decision-making framework to be deployed and used correctly, these six steps need to be incorporated in some way, shape, or form. The six steps are: ask, acquire, analyze, apply, announce, and assess. I am going to modify these from Kevin's work a bit and name them: ask, acquire,

FIGURE 9.1 Data informed decision-making

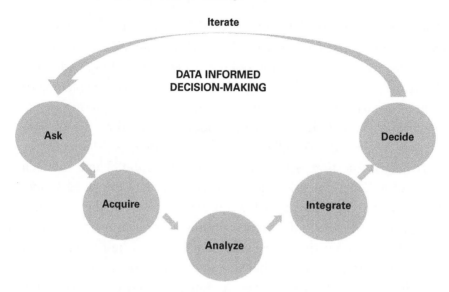

analyze, integrate, decide, and iterate. The reason for the shift is to clarify more, directed at each purpose and understanding. Look at Figure 9.1 to see the key distinction in this framework.

Do you notice something about this framework? It is infinite in its design. This is part of the design of data informed decision-making. As we roll through the process of working towards insight and a data informed decision, we must know that nothing is guaranteed with decision-making. This is part of the beauty of a strong data informed decision-making framework: we have the ability to iterate and learn from the past decisions. We never want to sit back and rest on our laurels with our decisions. We want to use our framework and our data literacy skills to improve upon our decisions and help them become even better. Statistics is a field of probabilities and sometimes probabilities do not go the way we want. That is ok, we learn from our decisions, the process, and more.

To help us understand the framework more, let us jump in and understand each step in more detail. Herein we will dive into the different angles of data literacy and how these angles help empower data informed decision-making. Then, to conclude the chapter, we will combine this into a full picture of decision-making.

Step 1: Ask

The first step of the data informed decision-making framework is 'ask'– to ask a question that needs to be answered. There are many questions to ask when we are looking at decision-making with data. There are also many aspects of asking a question to understand. To help us, we will look at the structure of questions through the characteristics of the definition of data literacy and the three Cs of data literacy. Afterwards, we will move towards the four levels of analytics.

Asking a question is not just *asking* a question. There is much more to it. When we ask a question within a data informed framework, we need to look at a few different aspects of the questions intelligently and with a data centric mindset. For example, we cannot just ask ambiguous questions, such as what is our best product? Or which marketing campaign that we ran was the most effective? These questions do not lend themselves to smart, sound decisions within data and analytics. To make these effective questions, they need to be unambiguous and clearer.

What is it that gets in the way of these questions working within the framework? Let us reconsider the questions from the previous paragraph, starting with: what do we mean by best product? Are all products of the same make and design, so the comparison would be in an apple-to-apple fashion? If not, what will the resulting data show? With our marketing question, how are we defining the term 'effective'? Could this differ depending on the perspective of the stakeholder? Do you see where this is going? Overall, when we are asking a question within our data informed decision-making framework, we must ensure we are asking a specific question that data can be used to answer.

Asking a question comes right to the forefront of the first characteristic of data literacy and the first C of data literacy: reading data and curiosity.

As an individual reads data, whether it be in the form of a news headline, information in a dashboard, quarterly report or a powerful data visualization, they should have questions. Here is a sampling of a few print headlines.[2] Would you ask questions?

- 'Missippi's literacy program shows improvement?' (I mean, we all should be asking questions here.)
- 'County to pay $250,000 to advertise lack of funds.' (Did anyone think this one through?)
- 'American Airlines Removes Passenger Who Won't Stop Doing Pull-ups.' (Where was he doing the pull-ups?)[3]

With each of these headlines, we should be asking questions – they are funny after all. Equally, as we are going through our careers and as organizations work through so much work and data, asking questions should be at the front of our mind. With the headlines, these are right in our face and so the questions may seem obvious, but with data this is not always the case. Reading data allows us to dig into the information and see what has been presented to us from many different channels and sources. This is where the first C of data literacy should kick in.

The first C of data literacy is one of my favorite words: curiosity. Curiosity is so powerful, as we saw earlier in the book. When it comes to making data informed decisions, curiosity flows through the first step of asking a question.

Herein we are going to combine another familiar term from our earlier data literacy chapters: data fluency. Combining these together, data fluency and curiosity, we can ask questions to determine what is happening and why, and use that to drive us forward through the steps of the data informed decision-making framework.

The four levels of analytics

With the first step of asking the question, our ability to do this throughout the four levels of analytics should be apparent, but if not, we will illuminate it here. The first level of descriptive analytics could be the starting point for most of your data informed decisions or those of an organization. The descriptive analytic is putting the data to paper, in small terms. As we put the data to paper, we can see what is happening in the data, when it happened, and we can start to tell the story that exists there.

Once we have stepped up and read descriptive analytics, our minds could be flowing with powerful thoughts and questions around 'why' this happened. To me, that is a direct recipe for diagnostic analytics. We need to keep asking these questions, but remember they need to be specific and unambiguous. If we leave the door open to ambiguity, we may struggle to find the why that exists.

Within predictive and prescriptive analytics, the third and fourth levels, within the data informed decision-making framework, asking questions may be all one needs to do with data literacy. For most of us, we will not be doing advanced, technical data analysis or statistics. With that in mind, our first step would be to drive data informed decisions by asking questions of the predictive or prescriptive analytic. Here again, as was mentioned before with the different angles of data literacy and data informed decision-making, communicating with data (the fourth characteristic in the definition of data literacy) and data fluency are at the forefront. If those who are not technical cannot communicate with those who are technical, we may fall flat on our face with the first step within the data informed decision-making technique. With this in mind, asking a question, the first step is critical to ensuring we get the data informed decision-making framework working correctly.

Step 2: Acquire

Acquiring data is arguably not the 'sexiest' step in the process. However, it is important within the steps of a decision-making framework, because how can work really drive a data informed decision without data?

To begin, let us make clear what we mean by acquiring data. We do not want to acquire just any data that is available, as that could make it hard for us to find the answers we are looking for. For our data informed decision-making framework, we are looking to acquire data that will help us specifically answer the question we asked in step one.

Let us say we are asking how well you played against a specific opponent who you matched up with just a few weeks ago and will be playing again in the next match. In the previous match, you were beat soundly in different phases of the game, so your data informed specific question is: In what aspects of the game were we beat and what caused us to get beat? Here, we can see both descriptive analytics, the aspects of the game where we were beat, and the diagnostic side of why this happened.

Now that we have this question in place, it becomes easier to look at the data and find the correct data to answer those questions, combined, of course, with our data literacy abilities. In this case, if we were not specific, we may have data pulled for us that is not relevant. We last played this opponent three weeks ago. What if the data pulled was against the opponent but from five years ago, when the team had different players and a different manager? What if they pulled the wrong opponent (not necessarily a bad thing, where we can say how we are playing overall, but that isn't the question we wanted answered)? Because we were more specific in our question in step one, we can dig in and find what should be data that aligns more closely to our goal.

With this acquisition of data, there are two key characteristics of the definition of data literacy that come into play: working and communicating with data. These two characteristics are key to helping us acquire the right data.

Working with data

For those working with data, acquiring data may be causally related to your work. If your job is to source and acquire data, or to build a data visualization, you may be working directly with data. This is a key characteristic and a strong way to work with data. You may have a role that sources data and builds data models as a data architect. Here, you are working directly with the data. Also, when you are asking the question and acquiring the data specific to your question, you then will work with it and read it as you start to proceed through the data informed decision-making framework.

Communication data

Along with working with data, the fourth characteristic of the definition of data literacy might be the most important when it comes to
data literacy and acquiring data. Are you the one making the request
to acquire specific data, and can you ask for the right kind of data?
Herein, the communicating of data, and data fluency, matter
immensely. If you have a question you want to answer with data and
if you know or think you know the kind of data you want and need
to answer that question, then it is so vitally important you can
communicate it well to the teams who will get you that data. Here we
combine the specificity of the data you are looking to acquire to
answer your question, the clarity of what you need, etc. I find the
ambiguity of data questions and requests to not only be a frustrating
thing for the correct use of data, but a strong impediment to successful data informed decision-making.

The four levels of analytics

Within acquiring data, the four levels of analytics come into play in a
similar way. If we are trying to build descriptive, diagnostic, predictive, or prescriptive analytics to work with or answer our questions,
acquiring the right data is necessary. Many times, when we build these
types of analytics, they are shared with various audiences across an
organization. When they are shared throughout an organization or in
other ways, if the right data was not acquired, it can spell disaster for
the organization trying to make the right decision. That said, when it
is done in the correct manner, the right data is acquired to build a
powerful data visualization, strong diagnostic case, and predictive/
prescriptive analytics that will help us answer our question.

Step 3: Analyze

Within this book, we have done much to describe what it means to
analyze data, so we do not need to go over that much in this section,

but we will cover it through the lens of the data informed decision-making framework. What does it mean to analyze data within our data informed decision-making framework? We will use the previous chapters to illustrate this within our framework.

The first area within the framework to understand is that with a good question (ask) we can bring to life the areas we will analyze. An ambiguous and murky question does not lend itself to strong data informed decisions. With the clarity that we seek, we are able to drive forward with the analyzing we want.

Along with clarity on the ask phase, the ability to acquire the data correctly is paramount to analyzing the information in a sound manner. Through the proper acquisition of data, we are opening doors for successful insight. Remember, insight is one of the main goals of data literacy. With insight we can drive decisions. If we have poor data, our insight will be 'poor' as well. We may spend countless hours building a brilliant data visualization, strong statistical model, and so forth, only to find out the data we were using was bad. What a shame! The correct acquisition of data allows us to analyze data and information in a better manner.

Within analyzing the data in the data informed decision-making framework, we are directly tying ourselves to the third characteristic of data literacy and the second and third Cs of data literacy: analyzing data (fitting, right?), and creativity and critical thinking. The third characteristic of data literacy is painfully obvious here and will continue to play the critical role that it has through the data informed decision-making framework.

Both creativity and critical thinking are empowering for an individual in the third step of data informed decision-making. One might not think of creativity when it comes to analyzing data, but that is exactly one skill we should be deploying on a regular basis. I have a strong fear that too much is lost and missed within data and analytics because we humans turn into 'robots' to analyze the information in front of us. We use the same set analyses, the same processes, and the same tools to derive insight. Unfortunately, this is not all we should be doing. In fact, when we drive insight through analysis in this manner, we are missing crucial things that could help us to drive powerful insight throughout our careers, organizations, and lives. By bringing in our curiosity with asking the question and with the data in front of us, why don't we try a different approach to understand the data and information? Why don't we push forward with a new idea and thought process? We should be doing this on a regular basis! We should be looking at things from a different angle. Another powerful thing we can do is bring in someone to offer a different perspective and idea. Maybe invite someone whom you would never think to be strong in data literacy skills and see what they think on the matter. Who knows, you might find exactly what you need.

Along with creativity, use critical thinking skills to drive the right insight. Critical thinking is such a powerful thing in our lives, but I feel in our world it is greatly missing. How long do our social media feeds stay put and not refresh? How quickly are news bulletins run across our screens? Unfortunately, too quickly. With the quick, 20-second sound bites that permeate throughout our lives, we do not possess the strongest of critical thinking skills. This is such a detriment to our lives. I long for the day when individuals and organizations don't just jump on the latest bandwagon, but we all take the time to sit back, reflect on what is in front of us, and truly critically think on the data and information. If we were to do this, we would be much more successful in our data informed decision-making work.

To conclude this section, we can quickly go over the four levels of analytics and their place with analyze within the data informed decision-making framework. We know that within each of the four levels of analytics, we are going to be looking at analyzing data. In descriptive, it is within analyzing data that we can move along the path of the four levels of analytics. Analyzing data is the essence of diagnostic analytics. Within predictive and prescriptive analytics, we must analyze the information these levels and models play in our decision-making process. By doing so, we are able to drive the decision-making we would like.

Overall, analyzing data is powerful for data informed decision-making and is our third step. When done properly, we are in a position to move forward to the fourth step: integrate.

Step 4: Integrate

What could I mean by the word integrate? From Merriam-Webster's dictionary we learn that integrate means: 'to form, coordinate, or blend into a functioning or unified whole'.[4] So, what would be integrating into our world of data informed decision-making? This may be my favorite part of the six-step process: we are integrating the human element into the data informed decision-making process.

Far too often, in the data world, the data and technology take center stage. When we allow the data and technology to take center stage, unfortunately bad things can happen. Do you remember the financial crisis of 2007–08? It seems not that long ago, but it is over a decade old now in 2020 and the COVID-19 pandemic seems to have put it firmly in the background. For a quick refresh on the topic, the housing markets were booming but there was an underlying current of, well, insanity if you will. In one of the most important models at the time, the prediction for a big crash was almost non-existent. Where were people as the balancing of this model? Why didn't people step in to help the world understand that something was just not right with the housing market?

Another example where data and technology have a bias in them that leads to poorer decisions is when the Apple credit card gave higher limits to men versus women. This has been seen in the banking and financial services industry, where an algorithm has come up biased or skewed for or against a gender, race, etc. Unfortunately, this is an area where the human element missed the mark and unfortunately had what I consider dire consequences.

The human element

With these examples in mind, I do not want us to think this is all negative, far from it. When the correct integration of the human element and data and technology merge together for a concrete and sound decision, the results can be fantastic. So, the question can be posed: how do we do this? How do we integrate the human element into the world of data and analytics? To do this, we will start by looking at different ways the human element needs to be harmonized within the data. Please note that I distinctly used the word harmonized instead of balanced. This is because we do not need the scales to always be balanced in a 50/50 ratio. We do not need 50 per cent human element and 50 per cent technology on every decision. In some cases, we will purely go with the data, and in some cases the human element may come into play more, but in the end we want to ensure we harmonize the two topics/subjects. One prime example would be in the laying off of someone from a job. An algorithm, the data and technology, might directly pick one person, but when the human element is brought in that knows extenuating circumstances, we may just keep that person on the team.

The first way we will look at how the human element needs to be integrated into data and analytics is through personal experience. One question that comes up often within the discussions I have across organizations in the world is: 'Are you eliminating "gut feeling"?' Within their careers, individuals develop a large repertoire of experience. This large library of experience creates within individuals a feeling of 'I know best off my experience' or 'This is how we did it last time'. I saw this in my career once. I worked for an organization that was really going through a rough patch. What I saw and heard at that time was 'We have experienced hardships before, and we will get through them again.' This organization was having a horrific calendar year, but the problem was the economy was doing very well. These wounds are what I would call 'self-inflicted' wounds, and so a new approach to handling them was needed. The organization could not just pull the same levels that it had in the past during other difficult years. Unfortunately, that is what I saw the organization do.

With our personal experience, it is not that we want to solely use our gut feeling to make a decision. We need to combine the data and technology with our experience. As we do this, we will find the answers can be cleaner and stronger, and help drive better decisions.

Internal and external elements

Another thing we need to bring into the data from the human element is internal and external elements. Organizational data is just that:

organizational data. If we look at things in a tunnel or silo, which means creating for ourselves tunnel vision on our data, we could be missing out on key elements that can drive catastrophe for our analysis. Think about being in a tunnel, whether in a car or walking. What is it you know about the outside? Well, if it is a short tunnel, then you can see the end. But in a long tunnel, all you have is the information around you in the tunnel. The same can be seen in decision-making without looking at internal and external data. What is meant by these terms?

With internal data, we are looking at the different things happening within an organization that matter to our decision-making and analysis. For an individual, it could be all the things going on with the individual in their lives. External data is the trends and macro-economic factors that can impact our business, lives, and so forth. For example, I remember when the financial crisis hit, and the world's economy took a turn for the worse. If I was only looking at my personal data at the time, not considering other areas of data, and placed myself in a tunnel, then I could have taken a wrong turn on many decisions. We need to ensure we are harmonizing internal and external data with the data we are using for a decision.

How does integrating the human element into your data informed decision-making work? How does it play into the different areas of data literacy we have been exploring? To help us investigate this topic, there is one more area of the human element that must be explored: bias. Just what is bias?

Bias

From Towards Data Science we learn that 'Generally, bias is defined as "prejudice in favor of or against one thing, person, or group compared with another, usually in a way considered to be unfair".'[5] There is also statistical bias, and we read later in that same Towards Data Science article that statistical bias is generally when the data is unrepresentative of the population. In our case, we are looking more at the first definition of bias. Unfortunately, in the world of data and analytics, our personal bias comes into play within our data informed decision-making framework and it is our job to work towards eliminating that bias. Take for example the decision on which marketing campaign to run. If we have a personal preference on which campaign to run, the data says go with campaign number 1 and you prefer number 2, you may just use your preference to go with number 2, going against the data. Do you think this happens in the business world? All of the time! By not eliminating our personal bias from a decision with data, we can hinder the fourth step in our framework and cause us to not make an intelligent decision. We won't spend an entire treatise in this book on bias, but I feel it important we touch upon a few different types of biases you may come across and hopefully illuminate for you the ability to get rid of bias as much as possible.

The first type of bias I want to help us with is confirmation bias. Essentially, confirmation bias is where we are looking for data to support our already held notion, idea, etc. Basically, we are not being open to all data, only looking for data that supports our argument. This type of bias is found all of the time: in business, politics, our personal lives. How often are we subjected to data from different sources and we are shown different 'answers', but those answers are tainted by the confirmation bias of the one delivering the message? Politics is the hotbed for this type of bias. This is where the politician picks and chooses the data they want to share, pushing their narrative.

The second type of bias I want to discuss is the status quo bias.[6] This type of bias is a very common one and makes us 'comfortable'. How many people do not like change and want to keep things the way they are? How many of us like to take the easy way out? In a data informed decision-making framework, be aware that if your decisions are going to look towards change, you may get many who just push you back and want to maintain the status quo.

The third and final type of bias to mention, although there are many, many more, is first impression bias, or anchoring.[7] This is maybe one of the most common types of biases, like confirmation bias. In first impression bias, we are looking at the first result, happy with it, and go with it. We do not take the time to work through and see if there are other results. This 'jumping the gun' type attitude can really hinder the data informed decision you are trying to make. What if the first result you run on a sales campaign predicts a 5 per cent return? So, you make the decision based off this, but later find out that the second iteration you run, with adjustments, comes back with a 12 per cent return? Unfortunately, your desire to hit the ground quickly can be a problem.

Within the fourth step of integrating the human element, we want to ensure we are bringing in our personal experience, that of others, and the organization, and balance it with the bias that may come from ourselves or others. I am fond of asking if it is possible to eliminate all bias from an analysis or decision? It can be extremely hard, that is why our job is to work on recognizing it, eliminate as much as possible, and notate where it could be in the process.

Within the four characteristics of the definition of data literacy, the four levels of analytics, the three Cs of data literacy, and more, data literacy plays a key role in the elimination or improvement upon bias. The more confident and comfortable we are with reading, working with, analyzing, and arguing with data, the more powerful we will be in the elimination of bias in our work. By doing this, we can become more confident in blending the human element with the data and technology element.

After we have integrated the human experience and data, the next step in our process becomes the big one: decision time.

Step 5: Decide

We have come to an amazing point within our data informed decision-making process, the decision point. Step 5 is actually in the name of our framework: data informed *decision-making*. We have to come to a decision. Herein, we need to remember the key elements in our framework of a data informed decision: first, we must make the decision. Second, we must let everyone else know! Third, we must get to work to put the decision in place. All of these are key elements in our data informed decision-making framework. As we implement these key decisions correctly and accurately, we must then ensure we follow those three key elements, combined with data literacy.

Within the definition of data literacy, there is one great, overarching thing we are trying to accomplish with our ability to read, work with, analyze, and communicate with data: decide. All these skills that we are harnessing and building up through data literacy are the power to make that decision. Within this definition, as we read the data, we are gearing ourselves up to possibly work with it more. As we work with it and analyze it, we are driving towards communicating what we have found. This is where we turn to our decision-making process. Of course, the four characteristics of data literacy are a part of each of the first four steps of data informed decision-making. In the end it leads us to step 5. The four levels of analytics really paint a strong picture of making this decision.

The four levels of analytics

Within the four levels of analytics, we are usually going to make a decision along the way. Within descriptive analytics, we are building dashboards, reports, and data visualizations that can empower our workforce to succeed with data. We must make a decision within these four levels that can help empower the analytical journey. As we use data informed decision-making in the other levels, we are using each of the steps that lead to our decision process.

One critical element of making our decision is communicating it. Can you imagine if a star athlete had sat down to make a decision, looked at the data and information, got insights from family and friends, took in internal and external decisions and made a decision to resign from their current team but didn't let anyone know? How would that be? Let me use the example of one of my favorite athletes who I grew up with: Michael Jordan. For those that followed his career, he made a decision in the middle to quit basketball and play baseball. What if he took in all that information and did not tell anyone? That could have ended in a fiasco. The same can be said with many of the things we are doing in business.

Let us look back at our tunnel. We can ask, acquire, analyze, and integrate into a data informed decision-making process and make a decision, then not let anyone know. Unfortunately, this looks like it would end poorly for all involved (unless you have someone who is really opining for your job). Instead, we must be vocal, make our decision, get the right parties involved and implement it. Here we come back to the fourth characteristic of our definition of data literacy and the power of data fluency. By bringing this into our work and the forefront of our decision, we are on our journey to a more successful data informed decision.

Along with communicating our decision, we must then get to work. I love my sport of ultra-marathon running! There is a lot of data and information that I can take into account to make a smart, informed decision on what races to run, how I train, etc. Imagine if I ask a great question: what race should I run? What if I choose a very complicated and difficult 100-mile ultra-marathon? That is absolutely acceptable! I asked the question, acquired the data, analyzed the training needed, integrated my personal information such as if I was injured and so forth, and decided to do the race. I even announced that I was doing the race on all my favorite social channels. What will happen the moment I do not get to work? I will have egg on my face when I do not show back up on my favorite social channels with a finisher's belt buckle (a common award for a 100-mile finish as opposed to a medal). I did everything I needed to do, only to have it come back to haunt me that I did not get to work.

So, as you put together a powerful decision and plan through the steps of the data informed decision-making framework, do not forget to do the crucial thing of getting to work on implementing your decision.

Step 6: Iterate

This last step is one of my favorite steps within the data informed decision-making framework to discuss and talk about: the iterative process that is data informed decision-making. To me, the term iterate means to evaluate, learn from, and keep going. Within data and analysis, and decision-making, there is one thing that is certain: nothing is for certain! If we are running a proper data informed decision-making practice, things will come back around, full circle. If you look back at Figure 9.1, you can see that it is circular. We go through the steps, make the decision, but maybe the biggest key is that we learn from the decision and keep the process going and going. Overall, this will help organizations to be more data driven and data informed. As organizations are looking to capitalize on the asset of data, they must be in a position to continually iterate. Thomas Edison, with regards to the light bulb, is attributed with saying: 'I have not failed. I've just found 10,000 ways it won't work.'[8] This is the same within data and analytics. When we make a decision and it does not go our way (I know, shocking that a decision does not work the way we think it will), then it is a learning opportunity and not a failure. How do we do this?

In order to drive iteration, we must have established a data literate culture. Within the book, we have spoken at length about a data literate culture. We must ensure our organization has a culture where data literacy learning is common, where people understand how analytics works, and they understand that the decision-making process is not a final thing, but a part of the final thing. With the proper culture in place, we have the ability to drive smarter decisions as the organization knows what a decision is, how it works, etc.

This culture is absolutely paramount to the sixth and final step of the data informed decision-making process. If we do not have the right culture in place, we run into a massive problem with overall data decision-making. Here are two prime examples of this, with one coming from personal experience in my career.

The first issue we can run into is that organizations do not understand that within data and analytics, the decision we made is not guaranteed to work. If the culture is not in place, with strong data literacy skills, then when a data informed decision is made, the workforce expects it will work. Now, I have not said we should not expect it to work, but when it does not, when we are data literate, we can use it as a learning situation and example.

The second issue we can run into is that organizations without a strong data literacy culture can have bias fraught throughout the organization and its decisions. This means, as individuals make a smart data informed decision, the decision might not even make it off the ground as you can run into opposition forces all around. Data and analytics is not designed to be a contentious field of play in the negative sense. Yes, we should challenge assumptions, debate on what we are doing, and push toward smarter decisions, but if we do not have the right culture, bias can push its way in and cause problems.

With the sixth step, the main focus is to know that as each decision is made and we work through the process of asking, acquiring, analyzing, integrating, and deciding, each aspect and decision will be analyzed, evaluated, etc.

Chapter summary and example

Overall, a data informed decision-making framework is a must-have for organizations looking to succeed with their data and analytical investments. Ensure you and your teams are following the process we outlined in our six-step approach.

The process of asking, acquiring, analyzing, integrating, deciding, and iterating should become second nature to you. This should be a part of how you work on a regular basis with data literacy. Again, without a decision, what is the purpose of data literacy? Data literacy should lead you as an individual, and organizations, to make smarter decisions. An example will help bring this to light.

We turn now to Rolls-Royce. Rolls-Royce utilizes the Internet of Things (IoT) and sensors on the plane engines it produces. These sensors are such a powerful resource for airplanes in the air, sending down information to the Earth as the flight is ongoing. Through this example, we will illuminate how the data informed decision-making process could have gone for the organization to determine that IoT sensors would be a valuable investment on the planes. Please note this is a hypothetical example of how this potentially could have happened, I do not know if this is even close to the real conversation. But this is an example of how the data informed decision-making process could work.

The first step would be to ask a question. Imagine you are an engineer or data scientist, and you are studying the external environment and you notice that the IoT and sensors are becoming a larger topic in the data and analytical world, plus the connectivity of the world. You ask yourself a question: Could we put a sensor on an airplane engine to relay information to the ground throughout a flight? There is step one, facilitated by your curiosity to ask a question.

The next step is that you think it would be prudent to gather a lot of data and information on the sensors, how they work, whether they could be put on an airplane, and if they could relay information through the flight; this is external data. You also study and learn about the initiatives internal to your organization, figuring out if the timing would even be right and how hard it would be to implement this on an engine. Finally, you acquire the data and information the sensor could collect, allowing you to paint a picture of this possibility. Step two, acquiring data, is complete.

The third step is to analyze everything. You did not gather all the data and information, internal and external, just for fun, did you? Of course not! You gathered all that information to understand and analyze the data. You sift through mountains of data to really put yourself in a position to understand the complexity, market, and potential return for implementing these sensors. You use your critical thinking skills to help craft different scenarios through your analysis. Step three has been completed.

The fourth step is to integrate your human element into the analysis. Not just your human element, but those of your neighbors, friends, coworkers, and more, to understand the potential impact of these new sensors and how it could help drive safer flying for millions. You are also careful not to get carried away with bias. You understand your personal desire to have these sensors, thinking the collecting of the data would be exciting and fun, but you are very conscious of the impact your personal excitement can have on this decision. Through this process, you feel you have integrated in well your personal experience and more. You are well on your way to a data informed decision with step four accomplished.

Step five is your decision step. Through all your processes, you have decided to put IoT sensors on the plane engines. You feel the benefits and rewards of doing so will greatly help the flight of airplanes, make the world more intelligent on flying, and so forth. You put the communication plan in place, helping the organization to know of the goals and plans. Finally, you get to work in the implementation of this decision.

The final step is, of course, iteration. As you implement the sensors, you are starting to gather more and more information on the sensors and how they are operating. Through this information, you are able to ask more and more questions. This gets you rolling on the process of data informed decision-making more and more. This is the power of a strong data informed decision-making process within an organization. It is not an overstatement to say these are critical processes for a smart, data driven culture.

Notes

1 Qlik (undated) Data-Informed Decision-Making Framework. Available from: https://learning.qlik.com/course/view.php?id=1021 (archived at https://perma.cc/32WF-BHD7)

2 Jenkins, B (2019) 25 Bizarre News Headlines You Won't Believe Are Actually Real. Liveabout.com, 11 March. Available from: https://www.liveabout.com/bizarre-news-headlines-4147212 (archived at https://perma.cc/B32Y-SXAV)

3 Renz, T (2018).25 Crazy news Headlines Around The World That Actually Happened in 2018, Thetravel.com, 25 December. Available from: https://www.thetravel.com/crazy-news-headlines-around-the-world-that-actually-happened-in-2018/ (archived at https://perma.cc/7V4R-36GK)

4 Merriam-Webster (undated) Definition of Integrate. Available from: https://www.merriam-webster.com/dictionary/integrate (archived at https://perma.cc/S6VV-4CGR)

5 Terrance, S (undated) What is Statistical Bias and Why is it so Important in Data Science? Towards Data Science, 18 February. Available from: https://towardsdatascience.com/what-is-statistical-bias-and-why-is-it-so-important-in-data-science-80e02bf7a88d (archived at https://perma.cc/RCT7-KE6F)

6 Stanghini, J (2015) The Most Common Biases in Business Decisions. Business2Community, 19 June. Available from: https://www. business2community.com/strategy/the-most-common-biases-in-business- decisions-01255194 (archived at https://perma.cc/M6KY-5QMQ)

7 Memory (2020) 8 Types of Bias in Decision-making [Blog], 3 January. Available from: https://memory.ai/timely-blog/8-types-of-bias-in-decision-making (archived at https://perma.cc/QB95-D2PP)

8 Ruth, A (2015) Thomas Edison – 10,000 Ways That Won't Work [Blog], Due, 22 July. Available from: https://due.com/blog/thomas-edison-10000-ways-that- wont-work (archived at https://perma.cc/8EZC-NX44)

10

Data literacy and data and analytical strategy

We have been able to cover an immense amount of information with regards to data literacy throughout the first nine chapters of the book. One area we have not focused on heavily is data and analytical strategy. Yes, we have spoken on it in various ways throughout the book, and we are not going to dive in from an in-depth perspective here, but I do want to touch upon many of the different areas of data and analytical strategy that I will call the 'hyped' areas. I do not mean 'hyped' in a negative way. I mean these are the terms and areas of data and analytics that receive much airtime in our lives, in our discussions on data and analytics, and in some cases are discussed with a zealot type mindset. I want to discuss just what these areas of data and analytics are and how they tie to data literacy. The areas we are going to cover are:

- data driven culture;
- business intelligence;
- artificial intelligence;
- machine learning and algorithms;
- big data;
- embedded analytics;
- the Cloud;
- edge analytics;
- geo analytics.

These, of course, do not make up the entire spread of a data and analytical strategy. There are many facets that can be a part of a strategy, and that is not to say everything *should* be a part, but we want to ensure you walk away with an understanding of these topics, how they pertain to a data and analytical strategy, and how data literacy skills can play a part within these subjects.

Data driven culture

There are few topics that have received as much attention in recent years as organizations wanting to become a 'data driven culture'. This topic warrants a lot of thought, ideas, and more. It also has become something of a mythology, as organizations do not know how to become an actual data driven culture.

In the year 2020, when the world saw things shut down in a heartbeat for the COVID-19 pandemic, organizations were looking to make the best decisions possible with many different facets of their business: employees and keeping them safe, helping customers to survive economic shutdowns, supply chain needs, digital transformation (as workforces were forced to become remote workers, instead of office workers), and more. These changes could be helped by a structured and powerful data and analytical framework, one where it had been working towards success for a long time. The problem? Most organizations found out quickly they were not really a data driven company, whether they felt they were or not. This caused a lot of anxiety and issues.

My calendar has been busy for a long time, but the moment COVID-19 shut the world down and organizations were looking for more, my calendar got even busier. I think that a lot of organizations played their data and analytical game much like an individual who is entering a swimming pool. We have all probably seen this or done this ourselves. We step up to the water in the swimming pool. We 'test the waters' if you will, feeling the water to determine its temperature. Instead of fully jumping in and immersing ourselves, we slowly inch into the water. As we inch into the water, those parts of the body submerged in the water get used to the temperature, and so we move further and further in.

Then, there are those who do not even hesitate (one of my sons is this way), see the pool and jump right in without touching the water to feel the temperature. Those that quickly and without fear jump in and immerse themselves are already set and enjoying the benefits of the pool. Those who hesitate or slowly get in are not there, and if they wait too long they could run into issues, the pool could shut down, or they may not receive all the benefits of the pool. This landscape is like a company not fully immersing itself in the world of data and analytics.

The term data driven culture is not one that has a set definition. We do not need a technical definition for this word or term. It is in essence the way it sounds – this is an organization and a culture that is driven by its internal data and analytics. I am fond of saying we want to weave the DNA of data into the culture of an organization. We want to empower the organization with the DNA of data and analytics. That is a data driven culture, one where assumptions are challenged, data informed decision-making is harnessed, where data literacy thrives. Finding an organization that is succeeding with a true data drive culture is hard. There are staples like Netflix, Google, and Amazon but outside of maybe a few, the number of organizations who are truly data driven is very, very small. There are far more companies that are wading in the water and slowly getting in, versus those that have jumped into the water no matter the temperature.

Because of the 2020 worldwide pandemic shutdown, this term and phrase 'data driven culture' gained more steam. As organizations were only tiptoeing into the water and not immersed, as the shutdown opened people's eyes to the realities they now faced from a data and analytics perspective, organizations realized they were not ready. The culture and workforces of organizations were not ready to pull the data informed decision levers to make decisions.

We have spoken at length about a data literacy culture in a previous chapter, so we do not need to address it here, but what does it have to do with data and analytical strategy? A data driven culture has most, if not everything, to do with a data and analytical strategy.

If we want the strategy to be effect and successful, we must have the right data driven culture, where data and analytics is woven throughout the organization and workforce. Data literacy is an enabling tool to make this happen.

I think sometimes organizations are looking at tools or the mythical and elusive data driven culture to be the strategy. Let me emphasize now: culture and tools are not strategies; they are enabling pieces. I use the analogy of building a house here. Imagine you want an amazing house to be built for you, so you buy some lumber, a hammer, nails, and maybe some other tools. You do not create the blueprint, but you expect it to work and be done. You then hire random people off the street and say, 'Build me my dream house'. How successful will you be? Unfortunately, you will not be. But now imagine you make the blueprints, hire an expert contractor, and get everyone onboard to build your dream house. You have a house building culture already in your plans. This is our data driven culture.

Make the data driven culture unique to your organization – it is not a one-size-fits-all approach. Some organizations are far along their journeys, some are not. Some organizations have a data literate workforce, some do not. Discover within your career and yourself, where you and your organization stand. Then, build the plans, blueprints, and strategy.

Business intelligence

We cannot write a book on data literacy and not include the world of business intelligence. To start with, we can turn to the history of business intelligence and the tools that made this world. Unlike some of the terms you have read about in this book which are recent, business intelligence has been around for an exceptionally long time. Microsoft Excel started decades ago. In the early 1990s, we had the advent of business intelligence tools like Qlik. As the future of data grew, so did the suite of business intelligence tools, such as Tableau, ThoughtSpot, Microsoft Power BI, Alteryx, and more. The list is much longer than what I have shared. So, what is business intelligence?

From Investopedia, we learn that:

> Business intelligence (BI) refers to the procedural and technical infrastructure that collects, stores, and analyzes the data produced by a company's activities. BI is a broad term that encompasses data mining, process analysis, performance benchmarking, and descriptive analytics. BI parses all the data generated by a business and presents easy-to-digest reports, performance measures, and trends that inform management decisions.[1]

Now, that is the technical definition, so let us put it into the non-technical sense. Business intelligence is the tools and sourcing of data that organizations can use to succeed with the four levels of analytics. Business intelligence allows us to gather data, simplify it, combine it, and utilize it in a tool such as a data visualization tool, utilized for analysis. Business intelligence helps us to utilize the empowerment of democratizing data to the masses. With that last part, we start to get a glimpse of how data literacy plays a part in business intelligence, but first let us talk about its place within the data and analytical strategy world.

Within a data and analytical strategy, there are multi-faceted approaches that need to take shape for an organization to succeed with data and analytics. One of those approaches is the tool suite the organization deploys for success. What kind of tool does the organization need to deploy for sourcing of data? What kinds of tools are needed to cleanse the data, for use on the democratized front? What kinds of tools are needed to analyze, visualize, and many other analytical aspects of the data? This is business intelligence.

Within the data and analytical strategy, teams are usually set up to help with the deployment and building of the business intelligence suite, sometimes referred to as the tool 'stack'. This suite is there to help the democratization of data throughout an organization, and to help the organization succeed with the four levels of analytics. This is where data literacy comes right into play, and if it is not present the business intelligence suite may not 1) work or 2) achieve its full potential.

As an organization builds it business intelligence tool suite, it will become very important for it to have a solid understanding of the four levels of analytics and how they will help it succeed with its data and analytical strategy. With each level of analytics, the tool that is there to enable the analytical level to succeed matters greatly. For descriptive analytics, we need the right type of dashboard and visualization tools. Having the right data visualization and dashboard tools is critical to ensure we are putting the right information in front of the right people. From there, the same tools can be good to help drive diagnostic analytics, plus there are those that can help us dig into our data more powerfully. The third level of analytics, predictive analytics, requires the right types of tools and software (and high data quality) to ensure the right predictions come out. With the fourth level, prescriptive analytics, the right tools, and quality are a given considering this is where the data and technology can help us decide what to do with the data.

Overarching the four levels of analytics are business intelligence tools that will help the organization cleanse, source, and place the data in the right place at the right time. This is an especially important topic for another book, but in the world of data sourcing and management, technologies are advancing and evolving very quickly. As they advance and evolve, the right people in the right position matter, and the right data literacy matters to get the data. As we remember in the second step of our data informed decision-making framework, we need to acquire good data for our decision-making process.

In business intelligence, data literacy is designed to empower the organization to succeed with the democratization of data. Business intelligence is a tool to help within the democratization of data in the data driven culture blueprint (think of our building a house strategy). Within the blueprint of building our data driven culture, business intelligence tools can be seen as the data and technology software and tools given to employees to succeed with implementing the data and analytical strategy. Does that all make sense? Basically, business intelligence is the hammer and nails of the strategy and blueprint.

Data literacy then becomes the skills to utilize the tools correctly for the correct end result. In our data and analytical strategy, the end result is making a smart and intelligent data informed decision. We also need the right data fluency through our workforce so it can help shape the way data is utilized throughout. One thing to understand and note is that data literacy is not just the theories and concepts that are utilized with data and analytics. Data literacy needs to also encompass learning how to utilize the business intelligence tools that are put at our disposal for data and analytical work. We can learn all the theory we want, but if we cannot implement it in a tool, in an effective manner, what good is our learning? The reverse can be true, too. What if we have learned all we can about a tool, but have no clue how to work throughout the four levels of analytics? Our learning can again be for naught. We need to marry these together to ensure we can be successful with both data and analytical work and business intelligence tools.

Artificial intelligence

To help us understand the world of artificial intelligence, there is an order I want to follow throughout this part of the discussion. First, we will discuss just what is artificial intelligence. Then, we can discuss its implication in the world of data and analytics. Finally, we will look at the impact of data literacy on artificial intelligence.

From Merriam-Webster's dictionary we see that artificial intelligence is defined as 'a branch of computer science dealing with the simulation of intelligent behavior in computers. The capability of a machine to imitate intelligent human behavior'. From this definition alone we can already start to see where artificial intelligence can come into the world of data and analytics, especially if it is imitating human behavior. This begs the question for me: can artificial intelligence make a smart, data informed decision similar to that of a human?

Below are some examples of artificial intelligence that will help illuminate what is meant by the term:[2]

- The use of Amazon's Alexa: In my household Alexa is a common tool to utilize (mainly for listening to music).

- Cogito: You may have interacted with the artificial intelligence deployed by the company Cogito and not even known it. From the company website we read: 'Cogito's AI solution delivers in-call behavioral guidance to agents and a real-time measure of customer perception for every phone conversation. Cogito is helping thousands of agents build better relationships with millions of customers.'[3] By using artificial intelligence, Cogito can help make our phone experiences more enjoyable and successful (hopefully).

- Nest: How many of us have seen this marvelous and powerful device? Nest is a digital thermostat for your home, learning and utilizing algorithms to drive heating and cooling. Oh, and by the way, did you know that Nest can be controlled by voice through Alexa? Funny how those things work themselves out.

Artificial intelligence is all around us in the world today, whether we know it, like it, or want to admit it. We have a responsibility to recognize its power and use it intelligently.

Within data and analytics, artificial intelligence has a powerful and empowering position. From the definition, we learned that artificial intelligence is trying to imitate intelligent behavior. What if we can get a computer or artificial intelligence to make smarter decisions for us in a data and analytical framework? That is power! Computers have so much more processing power than we do, at least from how many solutions and answers a computer can find versus us. Supercomputers can process so much more than a regular computer, giving them the ability to process and calculate many more things than we humans can do at any one time. Putting that power into the decision-making process is amazing and profoundly helpful. If we can have a computer working for us to make smarter decisions and powering a portion of our data and analytical work, we can see a greater return on our investments within these worlds, but what does it have to with data literacy?

The world of data literacy has an important and powerful impact on artificial intelligence, but I feel there is a misunderstanding about what artificial intelligence is and what it can or will do in the world. A personal story will help illustrate my point on data literacy merging with artificial intelligence.

I was on a trip to South Africa to speak at a conference on the subject of data literacy. During the trip, I made visits to different organizations to talk about data literacy, deliver workshops, and so forth. On one of these visits to a company, I was presenting to a smaller group of employees and we were having a discussion and an open question-and-answer session. A gentleman in the audience asked an especially important question: 'Won't all this augmented or artificial intelligence make us lazy?' Think on that question for a minute. What do you think? Will this make us lazy? My response to him hits home on my thoughts towards this wonderful and powerful topic. I want all of us to imagine for a second a dashboard or data visualization we own. This particular piece of work is one we have to prepare on a weekly basis and it usually takes about three hours to prepare the dashboard. Once complete, you send it on to the appropriate parties. Now, imagine that artificial intelligence is implemented in the organization, for that particular dashboard. What once took three hours now only takes 15 minutes. Do you just become lazy? No! You now have an additional 2 hours and 45 minutes to complete a deeper dive into the information or work on other projects.

To me, the advent of artificial intelligence does not make us lazy; it can help enhance our productivity. By empowering us with more time in our roles, we now have more opportunities to implement the three Cs of data literacy: curiosity, creativity, and critical thinking. Unfortunately, much of our work is not of the 'deep work' variety, as Cal Newport would say.[4] A lot of our work is probably found within the same, mundane tasks, email opening, and surface-level work. By implementing artificial intelligence in the work, we now have the ability to utilize our data literacy skills to succeed with data.

Along with artificial intelligence opening up doors of opportunity and availability, it will help individuals and organizations work through the business intelligence suite and/or the four levels of analytics. Artificial intelligence can be found with descriptive analytics, building dashboards and visualizations. In diagnostic analytics, having an intelligent computer can help individuals look and find new and improved insight. Within predictive and prescriptive analytics, artificial intelligence can play a crucial role as the power of computing and processing speed can bring about great predictions and help us understand what we should do.

Overall, artificial intelligence, while a bit overhyped at times, is a powerful addition to any data and analytical strategy.

Machine learning and algorithms

A close follow-up to artificial intelligence is that of machine learning and algorithms. Let us start with algorithms, as that is something we are all probably more familiar with. An algorithm is 'a step-by-step procedure for solving a problem or accomplishing some end'.[5] Basically, an algorithm will do a calculation or set of steps of calculations for a direct purpose or designated end.

There are many examples of algorithms in the world. One example of an algorithm is found within banks and financial services. Banks and financial services industries lend and loan out a lot of money. While they loan out this money, determining who is creditworthy and will pay back the loan is of the utmost importance. As humans, we have the ability to figure out how we can assess the worthiness of a potential customer, and then make a decision. On the other hand, why do we not utilize the power of an algorithm to sift through all of the data to find a concrete decision on if we can loan to certain people? Now, this type of work and algorithm can be good, but, like some others, it can be fraught with flaw and bias. Who writes the algorithm? Who sources the data for an algorithm?

I know I am over-generalizing here, but there can be issues of bias and flaw within algorithms. As humans have flaws or bias built in themselves, when they work on, build, source data for, and implement algorithms, those biases and flaws can creep into the results. These types of flaws have been found and seen within the world of algorithms and artificial intelligence.

A cousin to algorithms is machine learning. What does machine learning sound like? Well, it sounds like the machine, a computer, will learn. That is exactly correct! According to the MIT Technology Review, 'machine learning algorithms (see, a close cousin) use statistics to find patterns in massive amounts of data'.[6] Investopedia says 'Machine learning is the concept that a computer program can learn and adapt to new data without human intervention. Machine learning is a field of artificial intelligence (AI) that keeps a computer's built-in algorithms current regardless of changes in the worldwide economy.'[7] Essentially, machine learning is the field where algorithms are learning by themselves, and can improve for the betterment of our organization, data, analytics, etc.

Within our data and analytical strategy, and within data literacy, algorithms and machine learning have a place, but we must understand it is a very 'technical' space. It is powerful to have machines working on your side, learning on their own, and so forth, but without an empowered workforce that is able to use the results, it can be meaningless. In this case, data literacy is the power that allows the workforce and culture to succeed with machine learning and algorithms.

If we are working through our data driven culture and data and analytical strategy, algorithms and machine learning should be empowering the workforce, the human element of data, to have more time for interpretation, asking questions, and so forth. It should also empower the human element to make smarter, quicker decisions. This is where data literacy comes into play. As an algorithm or machine learning system works through the data, gives you results, and continues to learn by itself, you the practitioner had better be ready to utilize the data that is provided to you and make smarter decisions. Here we can see the power of the third characteristic in the definition of data literacy: analyze data.

If we want to ensure a workforce can properly utilize the data that an algorithm or machine learning shares with us, we need to ensure our data literacy strategy and learning are sound and efficacious. Herein we also see the necessity of being able to speak the language of data, data fluency, and of using the three Cs of data literacy. As we are utilizing the algorithm designed for us, our curiosity should pique and we should ask questions of the results, we should be creative with what the results show us, and of course we should critically think on the information. When the algorithm gives us information, we should utilize our power to critically think on the information and determine if there are flaws or biases in the results we are using.

Big data

The term 'big data' really came into vogue during the 2010s. The concept of big amounts of data is almost too good to pass up, right? What if we had large amounts of data that allow us to sift through, find insight, and really can help an organization to succeed with its data and analytical strategy? Seems like a great story and something every organization should utilize and capitalize on.

Big data is 'data that contains greater variety arriving in increasing volumes and with ever-higher velocity. This is known as the three Vs'.[8] The three Vs are volume, velocity, and variety. These magical words should make sense of how an organization can capitalize on the vast amounts of data that it is producing. In my career, I worked for one of the world's largest financial institutions. The amount of data being produced within that organization certainly hit the indicators of big data. The volume of data was vast. The velocity at which data was entering the organization was quick. The variety of data came from all over the world. Certainly, the case could be made that the data was 'big data'. But does big data live up to the hype?

Over time, the reality came to be that it was not only 'big data' that mattered, but small data, mid-size data, and more matter as well. It is not just big data that organizations need to capitalize on, but data of all shapes and size. If they are only focusing on big data, the organization can be missing out on the power that *all* data can possess.

Within the bounds of data and analytical strategy, individuals and organizations need to realize that they can get caught up in the hype of the data and information shown to them. In this case, I am speaking about the hype and hysteria that was shared around the world about big data. Within your data and analytical strategy, yes, you may need to source and have a system that can handle the expanse of big data your organization may capitalize on. Keep in mind, though, that your organization and you yourself may need to also source and capitalize on the data that comes in other sizes.

With data literacy, the result is the same: learn how to work with data and analytics and get comfortable with it. It does not matter if you are looking at big data, small data, round data, triangle data, and any other name I can come up with followed by the word 'data'. As individuals, we need to get comfortable with and be able to utilize our data literacy skills, the four levels of analytics, and the three Cs of data literacy effectively to find insight in the data.

Embedded analytics

The world of embedded analytics is a new and burgeoning field within data and analytics; I will add that it is also an especially important field that has emerged in the world of data and analytics. Embedded analytics is 'the integration of analytic content and capabilities within applications, such as business process applications (e.g. CRM, ERP, EHR/EMR) or portals (e.g. intranets or extranets)'.[9] Essentially, embedded analytics is where the analytics are put right at the fingertips of a workforce. Doesn't that just make sense? This has not always been a part of the systems we use on a regular basis, at least not in the manner and way needed. Embedded analytics is becoming a crucial part of a successful data and analytical strategy.

Within the framework of a data and analytical strategy, there are multiple areas that embedded analytics touches upon. First, we know that the world of data democratization is crucial for data and analytical success. We need to put data and information into the hands of the masses in order to capitalize on the amazing talents of the human element and workforce. This has usually been done with the business intelligence tools we have already discussed in this chapter, but what if we can improve it even more by embedding the analytics in the systems we use on a regular basis? What might this look like?

First, let us imagine you are a sales rep with a strong book of clients, and you are looking to expand the organization's client base, and establish new clients and stronger footholds with the clients you already have. Your organization is launching a new product line that you want to advertise to your clients, but you are not sure you know which client to advertise to. What if built right into your sales software was an analytic capability to filter, dissect, and understand your client base better? This would enable you, the sales rep, to make a smarter, quicker decision around who to target for the new product line. If this embedded capability did not exist, then you may have to ask someone to filter the data or pull reports for you, slowing down the process, and, as people know, timing can be everything.

A second example can derive from a warehouse and the stocking of product lines. Personally, during my younger years, I worked in a warehouse where the movement of product was of the utmost importance. Not just in supplying the shelves with enough product, but in the processing of orders from customers in a timely manner. The software we used would update on a quick basis, if input accurately (see, even if you are in a warehouse and feel data doesn't matter to you, it does), and we could see how many would be in stock. What if we had embedded analytics right in our shipping software and could see what customers might order based on history or we could see different analytics on our shipping process, empowering us to make smarter, quicker decisions with our shipping orders? Again, the power of embedded analytics is at the forefront, bringing data to the fingertips of a worker. The reality is, a lot of times the warehouse staff might not been seen as needing data literacy or the ability to have analytics, but this could not be further from the truth. When they are empowered, the whole team can be empowered.

A third example can come from my personal life. I love my ultra-marathon running, as you have probably been able to tell through the reading of this book. As I go about my training, I need to pay attention to the data and information my body shares with me. What if there was another powerful way to understand my training and how I was performing in my progress and plan, my ultra-marathon strategy if you will? It just so happens, there is: embedded analytics.

For my running, I utilize a smart watch that allows me to track my running in the mountains. It is so powerful in that it doesn't just measure and monitor my mileage and elevation, but it will also track my vertical feet ascended and descended, pace, cadence, heart rate (max and average), estimated VO2 Max, calories burned, and more. I can pull up my phone linked to my watch and look at what I was able to do, studying the metrics. I can then utilize these embedded analytics to enhance my overall ultra-marathon plan.

I think, through these examples, we have been able to see why embedded analytics are a powerful way to enhance a data and analytical strategy. Through the examples, we have been able to see how data literacy matters greatly, no matter your role or position in a company. With data literacy, you will be able to read the embedded analytics, work with them to filter and enhance, analyze to ask questions and get answers, and, finally, you can then communicate out decisions to others. With your powerful data literacy skills, you will be able to use curiosity to ask questions of the embedded analytics, use creativity to create a powerful story, and critically think on the information.

The Cloud

Here is another term that you may hear on a regular basis, especially as it deals with data. The Cloud is not some mysterious thing that exists in neverland. The Cloud is essentially a place to store and maintain your data offsite. Historically, organizations have held their data in data warehouses or other features, on premises. The problem with this philosophy and strategy is storing your own data can be expensive, as you have to constantly house your data and buy bigger and bigger servers. The Cloud allows organizations to store data in other areas, off premises.

Should moving data to the Cloud be a part of a data and analytical strategy? Absolutely! Some of the benefits of the Cloud include flexibility, reliability, a good investment, mobile access, recovery, environmental advantage, security, access, and monitoring.[10] All of these sound like important reasons the Cloud should be a part of a data and analytical strategy.

Data literacy plays a part with the Cloud when it comes through data fluency. The actual movement to the Cloud or knowing from where you access the data is not as important or as big a part of data literacy. You will still use your powerful data literacy skills with analyzing the data, regardless of where the data resides.

Edge analytics

Edge analytics is a new and powerful field within data and analytics. 'In brief, edge analytics involves collecting and analyzing data at the sensor, device, or touch point itself rather than waiting for the data to be sent back to a Cloud or on-premise server.'[11] We have spoken about the sensors and data collection of the Internet of Things. Edge analytics is taking the collection and analyzing of data to the sensors and other devices, versus waiting for that data to be collected and ready for analysis. I think that embedded analytics is a cousin to edge analytics. Here we see real-time and powerful analytics; game changing if you will. Imagine the collection and analytics that flights can get from the airplane engines or the safety and health power from self-driving cars. Edge analytics is a powerful way to analyze data, but what kind of place does it have within the world of data and analytical strategy?

Within data and analytical strategy, yes, edge analytics has a place. Will the majority of a workforce be working with edge analytics? Probably not, but it may be a part of their roles or they may deal with the data as it is produced, collected, and analyzed. Edge analytics most definitely needs to have its place within the umbrella of data and analytical strategy.

Again, as with the Cloud, it does not matter where the data is collected, processed, and analyzed, you must use your arsenal of data literacy skills with confidence, empowering edge analytics throughout an organization. Edge analytics has such great power, but like a lot of things within the data and analytical world, it can fizzle away for companies and organizations if the adoption of edge analytics does not come to fruition. In this case, use your data literacy skills to help your organization succeed with edge analytics. Do not let another investment in data and analytical work at your company not gain the return on investment it deserves because the workforce is not data literate enough to see it come to fruition.

Geo analytics

Our final topic in this chapter is geo analytics. Although this is our last topic, we have not created an exhaustive list of data and analytical strategy topics; there are many others.

Geo analytics is geography analytics. There have been great advancements in the use of geo spatial data and then mapping data into regions, etc. Here are just a few examples of how geo spatial data can be used to understand information:

- Understanding the movement of a virus and its impact. The world saw this brought to the forefront during the COVID-19 pandemic. As the coronavirus moved through the world, geo data and analytics were used to allow areas of the world to open and shut down at different times and places.

- Sales information. If you are mapping out your region, you can see where customers are buying and not buying. What a powerful way to understand trends and information towards your customer base.

- Crime waves. Using geo mapping with data and analytics, organizations can map out and understand where crime is happening, the kind of crime, trends, patterns, and maybe even use it to find criminals.

- Data visualizations. One way I have seen geo analytics work is through mapping analytics on a map, such as a person or body, car, etc. This allows us to map on different areas of a body or car where the data is occurring, allowing us to map, understand, and analyze the data and information.

- Supply chain analysis. Supply chain is a powerful logistics strategy, but can also have issues. Through geo analytics, organizations can understand what is happening in their very own supply chain and potentially where roadblocks are happening, quite possibly literally.

Geo analytics is a powerful addition to organizations' data and analytical strategy, and a unique section of data literacy. Organizations should utilize geo analytics where appropriate within the strategy, but not force it. Use it appropriately and where it can help, but just because something can be mapped does not mean it should be. This is something all organizations could learn: just because you can do something within data and analytics, does not mean it should be used. Figuring this out is a great skill within data literacy.

The same can be said about data literacy within geo analytics. Understanding and reading a geo map with data and information is not necessarily a hard skill to learn, but first master standard data and analytical learning. Over time, you will be able to adapt, apply, and empower yourself with geo analytical learning.

Chapter summary

As has been said, this is not an exhaustive list of data and analytical strategy topics, but it is a good list. One key thing this chapter should do for everyone is enhance their data fluency, a crucial part of data literacy. Within this chapter, we discussed such topics as machine learning, edge analytics, and geo analytics. Before this chapter, if someone had spoken to you on these topics, how well would you have been able to hold a conversation? I would love to hear confidence in your voice when you say, 'I could have held this conversation!' Unfortunately, most cannot. Now, using this chapter, expand your data fluency.

Not only did you learn about data fluency, you now have expanded your data and analytical strategy knowledge, plus data literacy and how it can be applied to these topics. Utilize this chapter as a framework on how to study other great topics in data and analytics.

Notes

1 Frankenfield, J (2019) Business Intelligence – BI, Investopedia, 23 June. Available from: https://www.investopedia.com/terms/b/business-intelligence-bi. asp (archived at https://perma.cc/MKG5-HPQ8)

2 Adams, RL (2017) 10 Powerful Examples of Artificial Intelligence In Use Today, Forbes, 10 January. Available from: https://www.forbes.com/sites/robertadams/2017/01/10/10-powerful-examples-of-artificial-intelligence-in-use-today (archived at https://perma.cc/J289-QZB4)

3 Cogito (undated) About Cogito Corp, Cogito. Available from: https://www.cogitocorp.com/company/ (archived at https://perma.cc/6BYK-CJYY)

4 Newport, C (undated) Book – Deep Work. Cal Newport. Available from: https://www.calnewport.com/books/deep-work (archived at https://perma.cc/4UXA-RWF5)

5 Merriam-Webster (undated) Definition of Algorithm. Available from: https://www.merriam-webster.com/dictionary/algorithm (archived at https://perma.cc/MES3-CS4Y)

6 Hao, K (2018) What is Machine Learning? Technology Review, 17 November. Available from: https://www.technologyreview.com/2018/11/17/103781/what-is-machine-learning-we-drew-you-another-flowchart/ (archived at https://perma.cc/EYK4-8JRP)

7 Frankenfield, J (2020) Machine Learning, Investopedia 17 2020. Available from: https://www.investopedia.com/terms/m/machine-learning.asp (archived at https://perma.cc/UBC3-JHGE)

8 Oracle (undated) What is Big Data?, Oracle. Available from: https://www.oracle.com/big-data/what-is-big-data.html (archived at https://perma.cc/7GGR-85DT)

9 Logianalytics (undated) What is Embedded Analytics? Logianalytics. Available from: https://www.logianalytics.com/definitiveguidetoembedded/what-is-embedded-analytics/ (archived at https://perma.cc/H77M-RHST)

10 Software Advisory Services (undated) Why Move to the Cloud? 12 Benefits of Cloud Computing in 2019, Software Advisory Services. Available from: https://www.softwareadvisoryservice.com/en/blog/why-move-to-the-cloud-12-benefits-of-cloud-computing-in-2019 (archived at https://perma.cc/TF52-FGPN)

11 Ismail, K (2018). What is Edge Analytics? CMS Wire, 14 August. Available from: https://www.cmswire.com/analytics/what-is-edge-analytics (archived at https://perma.cc/CAU4-MZ5J)

11

Begin your data and analytics journey

In this book, we have covered many topics and many areas of focus within data literacy, including steps to setting up data literacy and strategy. In our concluding chapter, we are looking at how to get you going on your data journey. We will cover data literacy as well as many topics on data and analytics. What I want you to get out of this chapter is three-fold:

- knowledge of where to start within your journey;
- comfort that you *can* do this;
- excitement for your journey ahead.

In this chapter we will look at the world we live in, and in particular the effect COVID-19 has had on it, to draw out key considerations for your journey. Similarly, we will look at how recipes are useful analogies to help us represent the ingredients and things needed for data literacy and data and analytical success. Personally, I love to bake, and if I put a wrong ingredient into my special 'daddy' cookies or if I measure them in the wrong amount, I don't hear the end of it. The same can be said for our data literacy, and data and analytics journeys. Organizations, unfortunately, have been putting in the wrong ingredients or leaving them out complete for some time. We will address this subject in this chapter.

Before we begin, though, a key starting point on your journey is developing the right mindset. This should be a mindset that the world of data and analytics will evolve, shift, and change on a regular basis. This is a topic that should have been prevalent throughout the book: the world is quickly changing, shifting, and evolving. More and more data is being produced on a regular basis. We cannot be stuck in our past and in the way we used to do things. We have to be on our toes, ready and excited to jump into something new. This is not a book on developing a mindset, there are many of those out there, but to succeed within data and analytics, we each have to be mindful and understand that it is a fast and evolving world. The stronger our knowledge of the future, data, and analytics in general, and trends, the better prepared we will be on our data journey.

The right mindset and knowledge of the future of data really can help us to implement a strong foundation and powerful start to our data journey. I am a firm believer that the more knowledge you possess, the more you will be prepared for your career. I also want to make clear that the topics we will cover in this chapter are also for your personal life. We are in a world that will be data driven for the foreseeable future. The more and more data we are producing, the more it will continue to be a part of our lives. Within the future of data, we are going to discuss a topic that hit and impacted everybody's lives and changed the face of the digital age and data and analytics forever: the 2020 COVID-19 pandemic.

COVID-19 and data and analytics

The world was thrown for a complete loop in early 2020. In fact, my personal experience with the worldwide pandemic and shutdowns was quite interesting. At the end of February 2020, I was enjoying a vacation on a cruise ship with my family, where I arrived back home on 1 March. Not long after that, my state, the USA, and the world was shutting down to help prevent the spread of the coronavirus. When this happened and shutdowns occurred, the world had to adjust, and digital and data driven lifestyles and workforces became the norm. No longer was there a stigma about working at home and things along those lines, as a lot of organizations were forced into this reality. Another area where organizations were forced to reevaluate the way things were done was within data and analytics.

As organizations saw world economies shatter and shift overnight, decision-making also needed to shift and become better, faster, and more agile. This was not just seen at the organization level; this is how lives needed to change. We as individuals needed to start making new, smarter, more agile decisions. In both cases, that of individuals and that of organizations, smarter, data driven decisions were needed to help in this crucial period. Unfortunately, what was found was that a lot of organizations were not truly data driven and prepared. This 'new normal' was here to stay, and it was a data and digitally driven world, for both organizations and individuals.

As individuals, how often were we bombarded by charts, statistics, and more information than we ever knew possible around the pandemic? Unfortunately, not all of this information and data was accurate. In fact, there are multiple cases where false and untrue information hit us in our lives. When dealing with something like a pandemic, nothing should interfere with the data, not politics or emotional bias. In fact, the World Health Organization called it an 'infodemic'. Now, call me crazy, but that sounds like a direct job for data literacy.

I have spoken and written on the future of data and analytics, surrounding the COVID-19 crisis, and through it there are a few trends and significant things that will impact our lives in many different ways.[1] A few of the key items I have spoken on are things that you can focus on in your learning and understanding of how you start your journey.

Data driven culture

This buzzword is here, and here to stay. Organizations were found scrambling and figuring out what they could do to be more data driven. Those levers that an organization wanted to pull and could not have become more crucial for organizations to succeed. Study and put time into learning how you can be more and more data driven. This may be the most important thing you can study – how you can truly become data driven as an individual or in your career. Each of us will have many decisions in our lives that can be enhanced through data, such as buying a house, the investments we can make to enhance our future, etc. As you start a data journey and learn about the future, focus thoughts and your mindset on what it means to be data driven. This should be a part of your data literacy skill set.

Data and analytics adoption

One of the biggest trends that came from the COVID-19 pandemic, impacting both organizations and individuals, was the adoption of data and analytical work. This is what I will call the 'New Year's resolution' syndrome. As you study organizations and what they are looking to accomplish with data, they all can talk the talk (so can we as individuals), but unfortunately they are not walking the walk. Organizations and individuals are saying they want to do this, but when the time came to see the results during a worldwide shutdown, it was not there. Adoption means exactly what it sounds like, to adopt and make a part of your workforce or your life, data, and analytics.

One of the best things you can do to start your data journey is to find where you personally have gaps in your data knowledge, experience, and so forth. To do this, utilize the power of assessments to find where you have skills and where you do not. With an assessment, you can then help to determine the right type of learning to succeed with adopting data and analytics in your life. Far too often, we look at what we have already in place, what strengths we have, and then implement learning on those. One of the best things we can do from a data and analytical perspective is to find where you *do not* have the skills you need, then work them in.

Along with this type of thinking on adoption, find those things that help you succeed or will keep you coming back for more. We can see this often in why our New Year's resolutions do not succeed, hence the name New Year's resolution syndrome. If you want to adopt something in your life, look for something you know you will adopt. If you do not want to build data visualizations in your personal life, then do not, but find where data is going to be good in your life and adopt in that manner. Yes, eventually you will want find those things you are not so comfortable with, but before then, start with what you can succeed with.

Data literacy

I am very happy to see that one of the COVID-19 trends and the future of data and analytics was data literacy. We have discussed this at length, but of course, as you start your data journey, put data literacy learning at the top of the list.

COVID-19 changed the world in many ways, unfortunately some quite tragic, but it also forced organizations and individuals to reassess their data and digital landscape. This helps us to evaluate and understand where the future of data will take us. We no longer live in a world where data and analytics is a nice to have. The changes 2020 brought to the world are here to stay and we must utilize the data and digital power we have around us.

Making a recipe

I love to bake cookies. Is there something you like to cook? You might be asking yourself: what does making cookies or cooking anything have to do with starting my data journey? In this case, this analogy is not only tasty but is spot on, helping you to not miss key ingredients to starting your journey. An amazingly simple thought process, but it has a profound impact.

When we are a baking a recipe of some kind, no matter what the recipe is, there is an order, steps, and ingredients to add into the recipe for success. To begin, maybe you must pre-heat your oven to a certain temperature, getting it ready for whatever deliciousness you are putting in it. You have to gather the right mixing pots or pans, maybe your mixer, and so forth. You also have to gather the ingredients, which in some cases means you set them out hours earlier to thaw or reach room temperature. Then, once you are set to cook, you follow the process or pattern of adding the ingredients into the mixer, pots, pans, and then into the oven. Even then, once in the oven, you are checking to make sure it is cookie right *and* you are cleaning up the mess you have just made. Once your recipe is done baking and basking in the oven or wherever it needs to be cooked, you take it out and enjoy it when it is ready.

To ensure whatever it is you are cooking turns out well, you follow the recipe and plan. When you forget to add an ingredient or turn the oven to the wrong temperature and so forth, does your recipe turn out the way you are looking for it to? Probably not! In fact, it could turn out disastrously. Plus, we should not pin our hopes on 'maybe that will be fine' when we are putting the recipe into place. The same can be said towards your data journey.

When we are making our first baby steps of our data journey, one of the key things to do is ensure we have the proper 'data journey recipe'. What does that mean? For starters, reading this book is a good first step towards your data literacy portion of your data journey recipe, but it is only one of the ingredients. We spoke quite a bit about the data literacy umbrella and the things that fall under its purview. We spoke about how data and analytics strategy matter immensely for the proper success in data and analytical work. In the previous chapter, we even added in some of the nuanced and buzzword topics that you may hear quite frequently in your data and analytics journey.

Through all these key ingredients (the four characteristics of data literacy, learning the four levels of analytics) to the proper pots and pans (the tools needed to complete your recipe), we have set up a smart and sound beginning to what you can look for within your entire data and analytical recipe. Some of the key pieces you will need to ensure your recipe is complete are:

- **Find a mentor.** Why would a mentor matter so much? One thing we did not speak about when it came to the recipe you were cooking or baking just a minute ago is the person who had to create that recipe in the first place. The person who had to write down what exactly it was you would be doing and following to create your delicious 'something'. In other words, there was someone before you who paved the way to that delicious recipe. The same can be said within data and analytics. There are those who have done this before. Those who have gone through the ups and downs of figuring out how much sugar to add or how many eggs the recipe should take. Trust me, there are plenty who have figure out when the ingredients to the data and analytical journey are off. Find them! Mr Fred Rogers of Mister Rogers' Neighborhood fame was quoted as saying 'look for the helpers'.[2] Find those who have slugged down the long path toward data and analytics success (I will speak a bit on this in the conclusion). They are there to help.

- **Invest in yourself and the proper tools.** Before picking up this book, did you have your own data suite of tools, such as Tableau or Qlik? Did you have a tool that makes data science easy like Alteryx? What about your own library of data and analytics learning books? The reality is, reading this book is a good first step, if it is your first step; it might actually be step number 11 for you, but reading one book is not going to be sufficient to succeeding in data and analytics. You must invest in yourself more and more. Some topics we covered that you could invest in yourself on are data visualization learning and having the proper tool to use. A lot of those companies will give you a free trial run, so test them out and find the one you like. Then, invest in yourself! Another topic we covered was data storytelling. What can you do to start improving your data storytelling? Yes, of course study, but also, volunteer to present at meetings or do some public speaking. Practice, practice, practice. Find opportunities to improve by actively doing the thing you need to do. We can read and study all we want, but practice is the key. Overall, investing in yourself and the proper tools is one key thing you can do to succeed.

- **Find ways to practice.** I just hinted on this in the last bullet point, but you must start to practice. We can learn all we want about baking a cake or shooting a basketball like Michael Jordan did or hitting the perfect putt under pressure like Tiger Woods, but reading does not translate into skills. In your recipe for data success, put into practice what you have learned. Whether you are trying to work through the four levels of analytics for the first time in your life and you have found an amazing descriptive analytic to start. You then figure out, or think you have, anyway, what is causing the descriptive analytic to be the way it is. You can then practice making predictions on what would happen to x if you did y. Then, reevaluate. If you have never made a data informed decision using a framework like that presented in this book, then practice. Try it out. Follow the steps. Practice makes perfect. One thing I want to note, though, is it is not just general practice. Anyone can go out and just throw up shots on a basketball hoop. I am very fond of the more recent notion of 'deliberate practice', which 'refers to a special type of practice that is purposeful and systematic'.[3] Don't just go through the motions, but sit down, find your gaps, and work through it.

These key areas are not an entire treatise on how to create the perfect data and analytics 'recipe', but they are a great start to things you can do to start your overall journey to data and analytics success.

Focus on proactive versus reactive analytics

To help us develop the right starting line for our data and analytics journey, I have mentioned the term 'mindset' earlier in the chapter. I am going to dive directly into one mindset area of data and analytics that everyone needs to understand and grow to truly succeed in the world of data and analytics: proactive versus reactive analytics. Please note, though, that both types of analytics matter, but we are greatly stuck in the world of reactive analytics within business and a lot of work needs to be done to help us get out of the way. I wrote about this exact topic in a blog article for Qlik where I started it off with the following question: 'How many of us feel like every time we work on a data and analytical project we are putting out a fire?'[4]

I could pose the question in a different way, because I bet this is something we feel regularly, even outside of the world of data and analytics: how many of us feel that the work we are doing is always to put out a fire or is done to react to something versus being proactive in our jobs? I find this topic to be remarkably interesting and one we need to develop a better mindset about for our careers, so we can truly help drive forward the right answers and solutions to solve many things.

When I think of proactive mindset versus a reactive mindset, my thoughts turn to Steve Jobs and Apple. If one studies the life of Steve Jobs, he proactively set the market and drove it, not just reacted to it. Yes, was it a reaction to things missing in the world of computers, sure, we can fight over the nuances of those terms any day, but overall, Steve Jobs set out and set the tone for the world. What was the thing before the first iPhone? It did not exist; the iPhone was the first. Steve could see the market, he did react, and he proactively set the tone. What about the first iTunes and iPod? Yes, there were things before it, but putting all our songs into our pocket was genius. The same can be said about the iPad. Overall, these great inventions were because Steve did not wait for the market to get there, he created it.

We need to develop a similar mindset at the beginning of our data and analytics journey. Yes, it is true that Steve Jobs was able to see the gaps in the market, react to them and proactively build amazing products, but that is not the kind of reaction we are discussing here. Have you ever been in a meeting at your job where your boss says: 'Look at these numbers, we can't have this. Hey Stephanie, go figure out what happened here.' Or 'We are having a fire drill right now and need x, y, and z before lunch.' In reality, we suffer greatly from reactive work versus proactive work.

In data and analytics, this is a very prevalent thing. Instead of doing amazing work on studying the market, the trends, and so forth, a lot of analysts find themselves stuck in a never-ending loop of reactive analytics, where a question comes in and they are pulled in to answer and give the reaction. Please note, I am not saying that there is not a place for reactive analytics. On the contrary, they are necessary at times and a part of the four levels of analytics. No, I am saying it is the mindset we need to be careful of. If we are always putting out fires with our data and analytics, we will never be in a position to prevent the fires in the first place. In other words, instead of reacting to everything around us and then deciding, we should be ahead of the game, using our data literacy skills, data, and analytics tools, to set the market and not react to it.

A superb example of reactive versus proactive analytics is the COVID-19 crisis. Over and over again, the world watched as different countries, businesses, and so forth were shutting down and reacting to all of the data and news in front of them. Sometimes, some of the reactions went too far in certain areas or cases (a whole book could be written about understanding all these things, and it is my guess someone will write one). Now, the world was dealing with something it had never dealt with before, so I understand that organizations might not have been ready to deal with this, but pandemics are not new and have been happening around the world for centuries. Could the world have been more prepared for when a pandemic hit? Could we have had things in place to ensure better safety not only on the health and protection side, but also on the economic side and with businesses?

Within data and analytics, develop your mindset to be proactive instead of reactive. Reactive analytics has its place and is necessary at times, but work towards being ahead of the curve by studying the trends and learning what is happening in the world. Build in yourself a mentality to be consistently driving proactive analytics, building predictions, and then refining your skill. Doing so could help you drive success by helping yourself and your organization not to react like all the others but be proactive and succeed.

Start with the basics

This might seem like a no brainer for most, starting with the basics, but it is not. I find it so interesting that many times as adults we are told basic things to help us succeed. This is not a new phenomenon and maybe the simplicity frustrates or annoys us at times. Within the world of data and analytics, and in starting your journey, focus in on the basics... *please.*

In the world of data and analytics, people get enamored by the nice, shiny object. We are pulled around by the wind of the latest technology, but in so doing we are pulled away from the sound and intelligent path that can lead us to data and analytical success. The data and analytical world is full of examples of overhyped technology or processes, thinking this thing will solve all of the data and analytical needs for an individual or organization. Such topics include big data or data science. These two were pushed into our minds and down our throats so incessantly over the past decade that they are somewhat of a myth, or people finally saw the light. In reality, both have a place and do matter, but they are not the only solution to your data and analytical needs. Unfortunately, though, organizations bit into them, thinking they would solve everything, and were left at the alter, if you will, when it came time for the marriage of data and analytical success with tools.

Within your journey, start at the beginning. Work on the fundamentals. Start by taking beginner courses on data itself: what is data? How does it work? How is data sourced? And so forth. Also, take beginner courses on analytics. There is no need to jump into the deep end and start learning about supervised and unsupervised machine learning if you do not even know what inferential analytics is in the shallow end of the pool. Do it from an intelligent perspective and start with the basics.

One of my favorite things to tell kids who are trying to learn a new skill is to look to the professionals. What are they working on? Do you see professional basketball players spending an entire practice working on the most elaborate dunk they have ever tried, or do you see them doing fundamental dribbling and shooting drills? Do you see professional golfers on the driving range working on the craziest bunker or chip shots, or are they working on the standard things that will improve their already supremely talented games?

The same needs to be the case with you in your data and analytical journey. Start by learning the basics of data visualization, how the tools work and so forth. Over time, you will develop the skills to build amazing visualizations that tell a story to help illuminate the insight you found. That day will come, but start small. Within analytics, start by getting better at reading descriptive analytics. Work to understand them, how they work, how you can communicate the story better, and so forth. Then, proceed and get better at diagnostic analytics. Learn to ask amazing questions of 'why' with the data and information in front of you. In so doing, you are able to absolutely progress and become advanced, but it will not be because you started with complicated things. It will be because you started with the basics. This is where your journey needs to begin.

The gamification of data and analytics

One area that should be covered within the data and analytics world is just how boring it is to some people. Yes, I said it. Do I find it boring? Not in the least! But a lot of people will gripe and moan that they have to take on data and analytics learning in their lives (I know, shocking, but it happens). The topics of data and analytics for far too long have been seen as intimidating and fear based. People did not want to jump in and learn these topics for fear of having to become a coder or statistician or, yes, I will say it, a 'nerd' (my nickname is Chief Nerd Officer and I absolutely love it). This type of mentality takes us all the way back to our math classes in younger education where we asked: 'When will I ever use this in real life?' This is a fantastic question, and the answer is that you can use math all over your life.

So far, my favorite request in my role working within data literacy has been from an engineering university in South America, where I was asked if I could help teach calculus differently. Such an odd request, but when you listened to how calculus was being taught at the school, you could see why the request could be made. Basically, as I recall, the students were asking: 'Where can this be used in real life?' The class needed to shift to an applicability and context-based approach to learning. This is not just this university's issue, it is an issue all around the world in data, analytics, and education on these topics.

To help us start our data and analytics journey correctly, we need to understand applicability and context. One thing we can do in our journey to begin and make it interesting is to gamify the journey. I am often asked when people complete my program or courses: 'Do we receive some sort of certification or badge at the end?' What a wonderful question! Yes, you should build out badges and certifications for yourself on your data and analytics journey. To start your journey, find ways in which you are going to 'entertain' yourself with data and analytics. How are you going to reward yourself when you are finished with a topic? How will you apply what you have learned after completing some section or learning? These are key questions to be asking yourself. You will continue on your data and analytics journey more successfully if you are enjoying what you are doing and not trudging through bored and uninterested. This leads us to the next topic within this chapter.

Find something that interests you and run to it

The world of data and analytics is vast and immense. Just in this book alone, think of all the topics we have covered. It was not a small amount at all, and this book is primarily on data literacy, not on data governance, quality, or strategy, which could have books all to themselves. This large amount of possibilities can actually pose a problem to us, rather than helping us.

In the world, we seem to think about having a ton of options as being such a wonderful thing, and do not get me wrong, I am a believer that having multiple options to choose from raises the utility for humans immensely. Sometimes, though, the vast amount of options can stop us dead in our tracks. We see the large landscape in front of us and do not know what to do. For example, my love of mountains and being on the trails is immense, greater then most I have, but when you stand at the base of a mountain, it can be intimidating and we can ask ourselves: 'How in the world am I supposed to do this?' Of course, the standard answer can come back 'One foot after another.' Yes, I get that, but understanding that does not necessarily rid us of our fear and intimidation.

When we see the vast landscape and power of data and analytics, and how many different options we have to choose from and learn, it can be overwhelming. When that happens, a lot of people will back off and go back to their normal routines on what they are doing and not even begin the process. Just like climbing a mountain one step at a time, we can begin our journey one step at a time. To help us do that, we should select something that interested us.

Data literacy, and data and analytics in general, are not one-size-fits-all. The learning, programs, and so forth, vary, and we as humans vary greatly. Because of this, find a topic that piqued your interest while reading this book, or something you saw on TV or in an ad, and start there. I feel too many data and analytical journeys do not begin because people do not know where to start or are overwhelmed. Do not be, and do not worry, many others have been there before you. Pick a topic that caught your eye and run with it. Remember, not everyone needs to be a data scientist, but we all need to be confident in our data and analytics journey and literacy.

Find your why

In this concluding chapter, we have talked about some 'out-there' thoughts when it comes to data and analytics. When we think of data and analytics, usually, we tend to think of the data itself, technology, tools, visualizations, math, statistics, coding, and the list goes one. In this chapter, we have focused on baking a recipe, having the right mindset, gamifying things, finding something that interests you and running with it. I focus on these topics quite often during my travels around the world, where I speak on data literacy and help organizations succeed. Do you know why I focus on these areas? Because it is my opinion that they will help a person succeed more with data and analytics than will the more technical side of data and analytics. If we focus on the technical, the mundane, the areas deemed as 'boring' then, well, they will remain that way and rising generations will not focus in on these things as much. I also find that by adopting these what could be seen as eccentric ways of thinking within data and analytics, individuals will buy-in more and adopt data and analytics more effectively. Once there, we can dive into more technical and 'harder' areas, but we cannot just jump in with our journey right off the bat. To help us jump into that journey, and I will list this as the last section in this chapter before the conclusion, but in reality, it should be your first step: find your 'why'.

Why does it matter that we find a 'why' within data and analytics? Can't we just go through the motions? Of course, you can, but how effective do you think that would be? Think about something you love in your life, anything. It could be a hobby, a movie, a book, your family, anything. Do you just go through the motions with that thing? No! Why? Because it has meaning to you and matters; it has a why. With that why, you focus in on it, you are determined to make it successful, you want to bring meaning to it, or a host of other reasons within this sphere. Within data and analytics, it needs to be the same thing.

The world has changed. The world of my youth and childhood does not exist anymore and we will not be going back to it, and you know what? I am more than happy with this! We live in an absolutely fascinating world, where the data and technology of today dwarfs what we had even just 30 years ago in the 1990s, and the data and technology of the future will dwarf what we have now. That is ok. The world of data and analytics is woven throughout our world now. Having the ability to develop skills in these areas is critical to your success. Being able to learn and grow in fields that will make you marketable for the future is necessary.

With these thoughts in mind, think about the topic at hand just for a second. What is your why? What is it you want to accomplish with data literacy and data and analytics? Do you want to use data and analytics as a way to create the true career you have wanted for years? Do you want to use data and analytics to drive a better life for you and your family? Do you want to use data and analytics to help make the world a better place? (Here is a *massive* hint: data and analytics truly has the power to transform the world, if we can but use it right!)

These are answers only you can give. You are the one who can tell yourself this is what I want to do within data and analytics, and here is why! Take the time to sit down, and write down your thoughts in a journal or somewhere you can readily access them. Doing so, you will be putting pen to paper, you will be able to drive solutions and answers. You will be able to find a 'why' that suits you. Then, you can start your journey.

Chapter summary

'The journey of a thousand miles begins with one step', said Lao Tzu.[5] The world of data and analytics is immense; of this there is no doubt. This world can be intimidating and frightening, especially if it is not a field you have wanted to enter into or if you would describe yourself as knowing nothing. But I am here to tell you: there is a place for every single one of us in this world of data and analytics. The key is to just start your journey. Do not hold back. Do not worry about being too nerdy. Do not be afraid of failure. Jump into the pool all the way and get ready for some fun. Let's do this!

Notes

1 Morrow, J (2020) The Future of Data and Analytics, Qlik, 10 July. Available from: https://blog.qlik.com/the-future-of-data-and-analytics (archived at https://perma.cc/KU55-H9FP)
2 Goodreads (undated) Fred Rogers Quote. Goodreads. Available from: https://www.goodreads.com/quotes/198594-when-i-was-a-boy-and-i-would-see-scary (archived at https://perma.cc/7ZKN-TGTP)
3 Clear, J (undated) Deliberate Practice: What It Is and How to Use It. James Clear. Available from: https://jamesclear.com/deliberate-practice-theory (archived at https://perma.cc/FLV6-NRPV)

4 Morrow, J (2020) Reactive vs Proactive Analytics – Shape the Future, Qlik, 16 April. Available from: https://blog.qlik.com/reactive-vs-proactive-analytics-shape-the-future (archived at https://perma.cc/BH77-RUXR)

5 Forbes (undated) Forbes Quotes. Available from: https://www.forbes.com/quotes/5870/ (archived at https://perma.cc/N2BE-88KD)

INDEX

NB: page numbers in *italic* indicate figures or tables.